101 LESSONS
THEY NEVER TAUGHT
YOU IN COLLEGE

THE ESSENTIAL GUIDE FOR STUDENTS AND
RECENT GRADUATES TO LAUNCH THEIR
CAREERS

MARK BEAL

Published by Beal Sports & Entertainment, LLC
Toms River, New Jersey

Editing: David Chmiel
Cover Design: Evan Carroll

ISBN: 978-1545362754

First Printing: 2017 Printed in the United States of America

101 Lessons They Never Taught You In College is available for bulk orders, special promotions and premiums. For details, call +1.848.992.0391 or email mbeal@ taylorstrategy.com

This book is dedicated to my wife, Michele. For 30 years, she has encouraged me to chase my dreams and pursue my passions, despite the time it took me away from our family.

ACKNOWLEDGEMENTS

I have been a professor at Rutgers University for five years, sharing lessons from a career in marketing and public relations. I was surprised by how many questions students had about their career after the classroom. Whether they were underclassmen or recent graduates, they all were looking for tips and tricks for navigating their transition from college to a career. That led me to this book, so I have to first thank all of the students who shared their questions.

Thank you to everyone who took time to talk through this concept, allowed me to reference and quote them and assisted in reviewing, editing, proofreading and design. I am eternally grateful for your collaboration and support.

I would like to thank my wife, Michele, again. I can't thank you enough for all that you have allowed me to do.

I would like to thank our children: Drew, whose entrepreneurial spirit is second-to-none, and his wife, Huda, the world's great daughter-in-law; Meghan, who sets the standard for client service in all she does; and Summer, who represents all the current college students who this book was written for and who will make her own transition from college to a career in marketing in 2018. I would also like to thank my grandson, Luke, who energizes me each and every day to take on the world and all its challenges.

None of this would have been possible without Harold and Audrey Beal, my parents, who instilled in me an undying work ethic and inspired me to pursue a career in public relations and marketing at a very early age. Thank you.

I would like to thank my other family, my longtime business partners at Taylor, whose collaboration, commitment to excellence and dedication to success over the past 30 years is something I hope every student will experience throughout their career. Thanks to Bryan Harris, who gave me my first break in public relations when he called me in 1988 and offered me an internship at Mike Cohen Communications. Thanks to Tony Signore, who I have tried to emulate since that first day of my internship in 1988 and who has led the incredible transformation at Taylor since taking over as CEO in 2004. Thanks to John Liporace who has served as a tremendous partner and confidant to me for more than 25 years in solving some of the most daunting business challenges.

Thanks to our "young partner" at Taylor, Ryan Mucatel, who keeps me excited and energized for the future of our business.

Thanks to all my colleagues at Taylor, who have continuously inspired me to evolve as a marketer and transform my career as the marketplace has transformed with the evolution of social and digital media. There are far too many incredible professionals at Taylor to mention, but a list of those who have collaborated with me for the better part of the past decade or more include PJ Brovak, Mike Costabile, Matt Adam, Zack Nobinger, Laurie Duffy, Maeve Hagen, Jennifer Knoeppel, Nicole Anastasi, Travis Rexroad, Jenna Mitchell and David Rodriguez.

I would like to thank my client partners — past and present — who have given me and my team at Taylor the opportunity to demonstrate our strategic and creative approach to solving their business challenges.

I would like to thank all the "givers" in my professional network; these individuals never fail to share their views and unselfish advice when I call for advice, counsel and inspiration. There are far too many "givers" to mention, but the list includes Stan Phelps, Gordon Deal, Mike Emanuel, Eric Liebler, Doug Drotman, Pat Scanlon, Ed O'Hara, Bob Babbitt, Mike Pierce, Sammy Steinlight, Keith Green, David Siroty, Jared Weiss, Matt Lalin, Jon Landman, Matt Van Tuinen, Jon Stern, Vincent Mallozzi, Rob Bronfeld, Ted Fragulis, Ross Kleinberg, Peter Hurley, Bill Holtz, Jeff Butchen, Matt Manning, John Gilboy, Bryan Kirsch, Bob Ciosek, Joe Favorito, Chris O'Neill, Rob Perry, Geoff Brown, William Nikosey, David Pangilinan, Tom Cosentino, Lenny Erlanger, Kristina Amaral and Michael Lasky.

I would like to thank Stan Phelps, best-selling author of the Goldfish series of books, for answering all of my questions regarding the process of publishing and the many details that go into authoring my first book.

Thanks to Evan Carroll for transforming my thoughts and concepts into a book that students and recent graduates around the world can read and apply to their own career journeys. Thank you for the incredible design and layout.

Thanks to David Chmiel for lending his many years of editing experience to this project. This book would have never been published without your final review and revisions.

I would like to thank David Dodds for always lending his creative photography expertise to my passion projects, including this book.

I would like to thank Tom Waldron who gives me balance in my work life by inspiring me with his fitness, exercise and challenging workouts each and every week.

I would like to thank my colleagues at Rutgers University who called me in 2013 to join their team and deliver real-world public relations case studies and experiences to their students. Thanks to Laurie Lewis, Steve Garwood, Brian Householder, Denise Kreiger, Jack Grasso and Steve Miller.

Finally, thank you to the hundreds of Rutgers University students whom I have had the pleasure of working with. You inspire and motivate me every day. I hope that this book can begin to return the favor.

PRAISE FOR 101 LESSONS THEY NEVER TAUGHT YOU IN COLLEGE

"This is the book we all wish we had when we broke out of the classroom and into the professional stratosphere, commonly known as a career. These lessons will get the young job seeker out of the gate fast and ahead of the competition."

SAMMY STEINLIGHT, FOUNDER, STEINLIGHT MEDIA

"It's natural for any college graduate transitioning into the work force to have anxiety about entering the business world. Mark Beal's *101 Lessons They Never Taught You In College* provides practical advice for individuals looking to turn their fears into competitive advantages."

JON STERN, SENIOR COMMUNICATIONS ADVISOR

"In *101 Lessons They Never Taught You In College*, Mark Beal has provided a great strategic roadmap to help young passionate minds embark on their careers."

JON LANDMAN, PARTNER, THE SYNDICATE.

"You really can judge a book by its cover, because *101 Lessons They Never Taught You In College* delivers exactly what it says it will, and more. After investing years and tens or hundreds of thousands of dollars on your education, if you spend just a few more dollars on this book, I promise you will be better prepared for the start of your career and beyond."

KEITH GREEN, SENIOR BRAND MARKETER & ADJUNCT PROFESSOR

"Hesitate not on whether you are making the right decision on your first job, but realize that it's the first step of many within your professional career. Be sure to listen, learn and grow through the experiences that you have. I had to learn Mark Beal's *101 Lessons They Never Taught You In College* the hard way so I wish something like this existed when I graduated."

DANIEL OAKLEY, CEO & FOUNDER, BTFL.LIFE

"Mark Beal is in a unique position as a brand marketer and university professor to offer real-world advice to today's students and graduates as they establish the foundation for a successful career."

VINCENT MALLOZZI, JOURNALIST AND AUTHOR

"Mark Beal has combined his experience as a 30-year marketer with teaching at one of the top universities in the nation for the benefit of every college student and recent graduate making the transition to a career."

ERIC LIEBLER, PRESIDENT, PROCAMPS

"This book should be required reading for every college student. If you're a freshman or sophomore and want to get a head start on internships, *101 Lessons They Never Taught You In College* will give you the advantage you need in today's competitive marketplace."

MELISSA JANNUZZI, RECENT COLLEGE GRADUATE

"Mark Beal is one of those people you want in your corner. No matter where I've been in my career, I can't tell you how many times I've reached out to him with a question or to bounce an idea off of him. Now, with *101 Lessons They Never Taught You In College*, many more prospective professionals will learn from him and the amazing wealth of talent he has surrounded himself with."

DAVID SIROTY, FOUNDER, IMAGINE PRODUCTIONS

"Mark Beal and I first collaborated many years ago on an amazing campaign that surprised athletes across the country with a ticket to one of the most famous endurance events in the world. His new book, *101 Lessons They Never Taught You In College*, is the blueprint for career success that allowed Mark to become one of the very best minds in the business."

BOB BABBITT, CHIEF EXECUTIVE OFFICER, BABBITTVILLE

"As a former student of Mark's, I can still remember his passion to help his students succeed. He shoots from the hip and is never one to sugar coat the real-life experiences that college students are so often shielded from. I wish I had this book, full of Mark's wisdom and wit, while I was still in college. It's the perfect read for everyone, whether you're a college student, a recent graduate or a student of life!"

DAVID PANGILINAN, SOCIAL MEDIA INFLUENCER

TABLE OF CONTENTS

PART I: FOUNDATIONAL ELEMENTS FOR YOUR CAREER

PART II: PREPARING FOR YOUR CAREER AFTER COLLEGE

PART III: INSIGHTS FOR INTERVIEWING

PART IV: LEARNING ON THE JOB AND INTERNSHIP

PART V: THE NEXT 30 YEARS

FOREWORD

BY TONY SIGNORE

MAKE YOUR MARK . . . academically, professionally, socially and culturally. For more than 35 years – beginning with the Jesuit influence at Fordham University and through to my day-to-day experiences as CEO and Managing Partner of Taylor – I have read, studied, analyzed and critiqued countless works related to these four critical areas. Certainly, there were many noteworthy gems gleaned from numerous experts and thought-leaders, but rarely have I ever come across an author who addressed, in a single work, practical advice from the classroom to the board room. In *101 Lessons They Never Taught You in College*, Mark Beal captures the essence of these foundational pillars in a most practical manner.

And just how did Professor Beal accomplish this in one quick read? Well, given my 30 years with this modern-day Renaissance man, I could wax poetic on why my business partner and dear friend is perfectly suited to pen such a valuable reference guide. But, alas, Lesson #37 suggests that we, "Cut to the Point," so I will heed his counsel.

In observing Mark very closely over the past quarter century, one might think he was born a leader, prepared to tackle any and all challenges from Day One. But I've always believed that leaders are made, not born, and this is clearly the case with Mark. Those who have been fortunate to spend quality time with Mark's family know that it was his father and hero, Colonel Beal, who instilled in his son Lesson #1 – Success is a Marathon – during this future leader's formative years growing up at West Point. You see, Mark has been a student and a teacher, simultaneously, his entire life, and it has been a privilege to collaborate with an executive who possesses such an insatiable appetite to learn. But it's the manner in which he converts knowledge, experience and theory into application – in real-time – that's truly impressive. And he does this over and over for and with colleagues, client partners and his expansive network of contacts, which grows by the day and continually pays dividends in a mutually-beneficial way. In Lesson #8: Never Stop Networking, Mark speaks of a systematic and disciplined approach to "connect the dots," as well as the need to "nurture your network." Advancements in digital technology allow those who are committed and focused to identify and align with key stakeholders. I have seen Mark master this in a way that has produced dividends on all fronts.

I'd like to shed some additional light on five specific Lessons: #4: Be a Transformer, #13: Hope is Not a Strategy, #18: Embrace Diversity, #44: Get Out of your Comfort Zone, and #86: Lead the Way. Mark recognized early in his career that while experience was critically important in moving up the ladder, he did not have the time, patience or interest to wait in line for a manager to determine what was next for him. These five lessons have been woven into Mark's DNA since 1990, and allowed him to take control of his own career just one year removed from college. At each level, he demonstrated an uncanny ability to transform himself and the responsibilities put forth by his supervisors. I would attribute this to Mark's willingness to embrace diversity of thought. This helped guide his way of thinking and continually placed him above and beyond his initial areas of expertise. And it encompasses more than vision. To me, it demonstrates the courage to lead.

As I approached Mark's final lessons, I paused and thought, "Here's a cat who has always practiced what he preached." To me, it's quite refreshing given the fact there are far too many preachers who have never practiced in the field. In closing, you'll come to understand Mark's rationale for publishing this guide for students and recent graduates when you get to Lessons #98 and #99. Having worked with thousands of professionals in my career across 60 countries, five continents and within numerous cultures, I have never met anyone more committed to "paying it back" and "paying it forward." And, of course, Mark saves the best for last with Lesson #101: Be a Student for Life. This embodies the man I have come to know, respect, admire and embrace as my business partner and life-long friend. It's a lesson that also reminds me of a very powerful quote from a truly remarkable individual.

> *"Live as if you were to die tomorrow.*
> *Learn as if you were to live forever."*
> -Mahatma Gandhi

Tony Signore
CEO & Managing Partner, Taylor

INTRODUCTION

I have been fortunate to spend nearly my entire career at Taylor, one of the world's leading consumer public relations agencies headquartered in New York, where I have had the privilege of collaborating for nearly 30 years with three other managing partners, Tony Signore, Bryan Harris and John Liporace. Together, we have established a culture of innovation, creativity, respect and diversity which I reference throughout this book.

In the midst of my third decade at Taylor and my career in public relations and marketing, I met with officials from the Rutgers University School of Communication in 2013. They told me they were placing greater emphasis on the study of public relations and asked if I would consider being a part-time lecturer. I jumped at the chance to deliver real-world case studies and campaigns at my alma mater, where I'd graduated nearly 25 years earlier.

Five years and hundreds of students into my side career as a professor I realized how important it was to connect with these students, who are preparing to become the next leaders in my industry. I am always eager to work with my students and the children of friends as they begin to think about their futures. At the same time, the youngest of our three children, Summer, was in the midst of her own college experience and was planning for her career after college via internships and professional networking.

These moments verified everything I was hearing from students across the country – that there was no comprehensive course instructing students how to prepare for the transition from college to a career, from developing resumés and cover letters to building a professional network and nailing interviews for jobs and internships to actually getting the job. So *101 Lessons They Never Taught You In College* was born.

From the first lesson, "Success Is A Marathon," to the last, "Be A Student For Life," this book is intended to be an easy-to-use "driver's manual" to help you avoid any potholes on the road to launching your career and thriving in your chosen profession. These easy-to-use lessons come from students and real-life experiences Some lessons are in response to the most commonly asked questions by students, while others come from colleagues or thought leaders in business.

I hope you enjoy reading *101 Lessons They Never Taught You In College.* Please remember that this is a resource, not a novel. So, when you to get to the last page, don't just put it on the shelf and forget about it. Instead, use it as a guide as you take each step along your unique journey to begin your career.

From establishing your professional network and meeting people of influence to conducting interviews and landing that first job after college, this book is intended to assist you each and every step along the way. Please keep it close by or in your backpack and pull it out as you approach a new experience in your career. Mark it up, recording your hits and misses in the margins of each chapter so that you can refer to them when situations arise and you could use positive reinforcement. So, let's get started on the path to making your transition from college to a career a more informed and rewarding experience...

PART I

FOUNDATIONAL ELEMENTS FOR YOUR CAREER

LESSON 1

SUCCESS IS A MARATHON

If I had a dollar for every student who was simply looking for the short-term satisfaction of getting hired by the time they graduate, I would be writing this book from my compound in Bali.

Yes, that first job is important, but it is more important to make a commitment and invest in your professional development. It is hard to take the long view when you are 22-years-old, but your professional journey is a marathon and your first job is, for most people, the first 100 yards.

It may be hard to tell your friends and your judgmental Aunt Edna to believe you when you say with a straight face, "I am waiting for the right opportunity. My professional development is a long journey and the finish line is more than 30 years in the distance." But trust me... I have run five marathons and I draw many parallels between the methodical training necessary to successfully complete a marathon and the process of establishing and evolving over the course of a successful career.

You have spent four years in college, so it's no surprise that you feel anxious to work. But try to embrace this journey, because when you find value in every networking meeting and interview, you will begin to see these new connections as the first step in developing long-term relationships with potential mentors who will provide their valuable time, contacts, guidance, counsel and maybe even an opening to that first job if you make a sincere long-term investment and commitment to your career.

MAKE YOUR MARK

Start building your network in college, be curious and learn from family, friends and friends of friends. People want to help, but they want to help you. Don't let mom and dad talk for you, so get the contact, make the call and ask for guidance.

LESSON 2

ENJOY YOUR JOURNEY

When I ran my first marathon, I had one goal – cross the finish line. I never took time to enjoy a single step along the journey. Finally, when I prepared to run my fifth marathon – in Boston – I celebrated every training run, new pair of running shoes and other milestones, big and small. So immerse yourself in your first professional networking and job search "marathon" as if it is your fifth... enjoy each and every moment (even the stressful ones).

There are two kinds of interviews: Informational (no job available; learn as much about them as they do about you) or Employment Opportunity (available job). Go on every interview you can get; do your research and make it impossible for them not to want you. When you receive a call back for a second interview, celebrate it.

There will be many bumps along the way, but take a positive and optimistic approach to your search. Make it an adventure, not a chore. Your positive attitude and air of professionalism will be infectious and make hiring professionals see you as a good fit for their organization.

MAKE YOUR MARK

Have a positive mindset as you take the journey from college to a career. You are only going to make this major transition once in your life so embrace it to the fullest and celebrate the small and big victories along the way.

LESSON 3

CREATE YOUR OWN RULES

In college, you learn theoretical concepts that serve as building blocks for your career. I am confident, though, that you got little practical guidance on starting your professional life. On the day you graduate, they don't give you a roadmap for the path to employment enlightenment. That's the reason I wrote this book, to instill in you the confidence and freedom to chart the course for your own unique journey.

You can learn from the experiences of others, especially peers who have found employment and mentors who have built impressive careers, but no two employment paths are identical. You are building your own career superhighway, so create your rules, test new approaches to career development. Try out a strategy or tactic. If it works, stick with it; if it doesn't, try something new.

MAKE YOUR MARK

Set your own rules for your career to go places that no one has ever gone before. Embrace this energizing and exciting time in your life!

LESSON 4

BE A TRANSFORMER

In a leadership course I teach, we discuss the power of transformational leaders – the visionaries who are never satisfied with success and are always thinking about how to evolve, personally and organizationally.

Grad Conn, Microsoft's Chief Marketing Officer, said it best: "Learning is probably the most important currency you can have as a human. Companies will continue to hire and to value employees who can transform[1]."

It is hard to imagine now, but you are on the verge of significant transformation. When you graduate from college, set the tone or theme for your career by being ready to keep learning about yourself and continuously delivering incremental value to every organization you join.

Transformative leaders collaborate with colleagues and create change for the better, all while setting a vision for the organization and working with their team to live and fulfill that vision. As a young executive, all you can do is find a way to stand out. If you inherit "boring" tasks and assignments that other entry-level executives can't wait to hand off to you, accept the challenge and make a difference. In other words, take routine projects and find creative solutions. If you make a transformative change with the smallest assignment, you will earn the respect of others and will find yourself being tasked with new opportunities, giving you more chances to make a difference.

---

1. "Lessons In Leadership" (2017, February); Fast Company, (212), 52-53.

MAKE YOUR MARK

You are not the first employee to get projects that aren't sexy and you won't be the last. But the quicker you embrace them – and reinvent the process – the sooner you will be moved onto more meaningful opportunities.

LESSON 5

CONSISTENCY ROCKS!

I have hired and worked with many interns and executives who have demonstrated flashes of excellence. And each present different challenges.

When I see an intern shine and then stumble, I can mentor them to see if they are capable of sustained excellence and set them on the right path to success. But when I see an executive who has peaks and valleys in their performance, I worry that they might have hit their ceiling and aren't interesting in developing.

To enjoy the success in your professional marathon, take a long view. Show up every day with an insatiable desire to produce high-quality work, day in and day out. Whether it's your first internship or your first paid job, commit to making a consistent difference.

MAKE YOUR MARK

All baseball fans have a love-hate relationship with their slugger. He might hit home runs, but he strikes out three times between dingers. Instead, be the skilled hitter who helps the team in every at-bat to be in control of your future.

LESSON 6

WORK WITH THE BEST TO BE THE BEST

Todd Rovak, CEO of Fahrenheit 212, a consulting firm, was quoted in The New York Times delivering advice to college graduates, "Surround yourself with people who challenge you. It doesn't matter what the job is. Just put yourself in that environment as fast as possible[2]."

Take Rovak's advice and run – all the way to the C-Suite! Every day, seek out the brightest minds, the iconoclasts, the big-idea strategists who will make you think, who will make you question what you thought you knew. They will make you smarter, more strategic and more creative than you were the day before. Make progress every day, even if it makes you uncomfortable; it will spur you to test yourself and empower you to evolve in your career.

MAKE YOUR MARK

Put your ego on the shelf, seek out the big brains, and put yourself in a position to question everything – every day – and learn something new.

---

2. Bryant, A. (2017, February 10). Todd Rovak On Turning Tough Days Into Good Ones . Retrieved from https://www.nytimes.com/2017/02/10/business/todd-rovak-corner-office-capgemini.html?_r=0

LESSON 7

WORK HARD TO MEET PEOPLE

David Siroty, a 30-year public relations veteran whose roster of clients has ranged from athletes to real estate agents, delivered a 60-minute lesson called "Work Hard To Meet People" to my "Principles of Public Relations" students – and it made me think.

I had spent countless hours stressing the same message to students and new graduates, but I had never distilled it to that simple five-word message. Siroty challenged my students to establish and grow their professional networks by taking every opportunity to meet and engage individuals of influence. From backyard barbecues and family gatherings to community volunteering and internships, you have the chance to meet someone who can support your career pursuit. The key is to be proactive in your search – and be professional in your follow-up. Get away from your smartphone, extend your hand, introduce yourself and engage in conversation. It will set you apart from other jobseekers and leave a positive and lasting impression with your new acquaintances.

MAKE YOUR MARK

It costs you nothing to start a conversation or exchange business cards with someone you just met. Don't hesitate to make a new friend or connection. It will pay great dividends.

LESSON 8

NEVER STOP NETWORKING

Once you get in the habit of connecting with people, take the time to get to know who you've been talking to and see how, or if, they can help you. After 30 years in the business, it never surprises me how small an industry really is. I can guarantee you that someone you intern or work with today will play a decision making role in a job or new business opportunity you are trying to secure many years from now.

John Liporace, my business partner of more than 25 years, has taken networking to a new level. John believes that young people need to get in the habit of networking, so when he started the JLS Foundation 13 years ago in memory of his dad, he provided professional networking to high school students in his hometown of Hoosick Falls, NY.

Once you meet someone, connect the dots and expand your network. In sports, there is a common expression, the "coaching tree." At the top of the tree is a highly successful coach; the branches are comprised of other coaches who have played for, coached with or have been mentored by that coach and followed in that coach's footsteps. Once you meet someone of influence, proactively explore other professionals who comprise their network. LinkedIn makes this approach to networking efficient, but it's up to you to be active in building and nurturing those connections to grow your network.

Once you start connecting with people who can help you, keep the conversation cordial and professional. Don't badger them to make time for you or endorse you for a position if you have yet to talk.

Connect with them as people and nurture your network. Call to check-in or write them an email just to "talk shop" or discuss something important to them.

If you only call when you need something, you might find your calls going straight to voicemail. Reward their networking on your behalf by being professional and engaged with the men and women they connect you to.

MAKE YOUR MARK

Most people are hardwired to help, but networking is a two-way street. Build a reputation as a facilitator, connecting friends and peers with someone who can help them. It will pay dividends in the long run for you too.

LESSON 9

RECRUIT YOUR 'RABBIS'

Professional sports and entertainment public relations executive Sammy Steinlight has served as one of my guest lecturers every semester that I have taught. One of Steinlight's consistent recommendations to students is to find a "rabbi." He is not suggesting they convert to Judaism. Instead, he is using an old-school term to encourage students to identify and engage with experienced men and women who can help them avoid any potholes and pitfalls along the way.

As you approach your junior and senior years, identify individuals – a professor, internship supervisor, relative or family friend – who can serve in this role of mentor and counselor. This is someone you already know, trust and have a collaborative relationship with. It is important to not only formally recruit your mentor but officially invite them to serve in this role knowing this will be an ongoing mutually beneficial relationship. Once you get into your chosen field, finding mentors who can offer industry-specific advice is a strategic long-term approach to investing in your career and nurture relationships that will produce dividends for many years to come.

MAKE YOUR MARK

You chose your rabbis because they have a lot of wisdom, right? So keep notebooks full of their insights and review them often to turn their words into productive actions.

LESSON 10

MAKE CAREER DECISIONS THAT ARE BEST FOR YOU

Whenever a young executive asks for my guidance about making a job change after a few years, I tell them that they have to focus on one thing: "Is it good for you?"

It is no different for you. Does this change help your personal brand? Will it help you grow and evolve in your profession? Will it help make your next career step easier? At the end of the day, you have to look in the mirror and make decisions about your career that are best for you – especially as a young person unbound by family obligations.

You don't have to make the decision in a vacuum. Seek counsel and advice from family, friends and mentors, Make lists of pros and cons. Then see this through the simple "success is a marathon – and this is my marathon" perspective. The decisions that you make will be the best for you, based on your long-term career goals and objectives.

MAKE YOUR MARK

Money isn't everything – yet. Don't let anyone else's concerns about salary, location and the size of a company from your peers influence what is best for you. Taking an internship after graduation may be the best decision for you, even if it pays considerably less than another full-time opportunity.

LESSON 11

EMBRACE 'UNSPECTACULAR' PREPARATION

My business partner of 30 years, Tony Signore, Taylor's Chief Executive Officer, consistently reinforces the immense value of "unspectacular" preparation. Like an athlete who rises before sunrise to train when no one is watching and the cameras are not on, the athlete prepares for their next opponent in a way that is unspectacular.

Tony reminds young executives that unspectacular preparation is what they must do after hours or on the weekend to better understand their business, the industry and the competition. In my many years of getting ready for a new business presentation, my unspectacular preparation was spending hours on weekends visiting retail locations, fast-food restaurants or auto dealers so that I could understand the products and experiences of our potential clients and deliver fresh insights during our pitches to them.

When you get in the habit of doing unspectacular preparation, you will set yourself apart from others at your level and deliver business impact that will be recognized by managers and supervisors who already know the value of this tactic.

MAKE YOUR MARK

Thomas Edison said, "Genius is 90 percent perspiration and 10 percent inspiration." Worked out pretty well for him, right?

LESSON 12

ALWAYS BE ACCOUNTABLE

Did you "kill it" in that interview? Pat yourself on the back. Did you find a typo on your resumé, three minutes before an interview? Own your mistake. Have one week to finish your first professional product? Spend every waking minute refining it, then submit it a day early.

In short, be accountable for everything you do, good or bad. If you blew an interview because you didn't do your research, make that the last time you go into a situation unprepared. Every promotion you earn raises the stakes; prove that you can handle increased responsibilities, manage a team and bring a project in under budget with no drama. Then do it again the next time you are asked. Be competent, make your supervisors and clients happy and set yourself on the right path for the remainder of your career.

MAKE YOUR MARK

Legendary football coach Lou Holtz said, "If you are going to pull your helmet off when you make a great play, do the same thing when you fumble." That is football talk for, "If you are ready to take the credit, be willing to accept blame, too."

LESSON 13

HOPE IS NOT A STRATEGY

In 2003, sales consultant and author Rick Page wrote Hope Is Not A Strategy, a book that focused on preparation as the essential element for closing business deals.

That mantra applies to every facet of your life, in and out of the office. Hard work, not hope, will earn you that internship. Anything you want is worth working for. If you are going to leave your future to fate, your future will involve a lot of ramen noodles and sitcoms instead of client dinners and business trips.

The lessons in this book have one purpose: To help you meet, and exceed, your career-development goals. Use these 101 common-sense tips and tactics to control many of the factors that will contribute to your seamless and successful transition from college to career. You can look up and down the table of contents many times and find that "hope" is not among them. That said, I do "hope" that you accept this lesson and are willing to take control of your career trajectory.

MAKE YOUR MARK

The more you prepare, the less you will rely on hope. Do the hard work and accept the opportunities that will come your way.

LESSON 14

DO THE 'WRITE' THING

I suffered what I considered a professional slap in the face as a young executive when one of my clients ordered me to take a business-writing course. I was a journalism major in college! I wrote for a daily newspaper! What the hell made him think he could talk to me like that?

More than 25 years later, I owe that client my career. I still apply lessons from that writing course to my writing today. No matter what profession you pursue, if you can communicate efficiently, with style and clarity – whether in a simple email, a PowerPoint presentation or 20-page white paper or a thank-you note to a client – you will stand out from the rest of your peers.

I review hundreds of writing samples from students and executives in my role with Taylor. I am sorry to report that, with each passing year, the quality of writing I see gets worse. I am shocked that most people no longer seem to put a premium on honing their writing skills.

If I were writing a letter to my 22-year-old self, I would remind me that I've got a long career ahead and that being a great writer will help me build a successful career. I didn't write that letter to me, so I am writing it to you. Work on your craft and you will win in business.

MAKE YOUR MARK

Ths isn't kmooniktng. You will be writing for the rest of your career, so lose the texting language and become proficient so that writing like a professional never feels like a chore. Ask any good writer how they got that way and they will say, "Because I read."

LESSON 15

WORK ON YOUR WEAKNESSES

From your first internship to your first job – and every job after that, ask your supervisors to provide constructive criticism. If there is no formal review process in place, set yourself apart by requesting regular reviews. While we all like to hear compliments and praise, the greatest feedback we can receive is to learn what our supervisors perceive as areas for improvement. Your bosses will respect your dedication to improving your craft, so take that honest feedback and set measurable goals to transform weaknesses into strengths.

MAKE YOUR MARK

Be honest with yourself, spot your weaknesses and fix them – and don't be defensive. You asked for the input, so don't take it personally when they offer insight.

LESSON 16

PURSUE THE ELUSIVE 'PERFECT' PRESENTATION

From your first day on the job until your last in the corner office, you will spend a huge chunk of your career presenting to audiences. Whether you are trying to connect with one person or a packed auditorium for the next three decades, it will be essential for you to perfect your presentation skills, merging impeccable delivery and personal flair to make information come to life. Practice your craft to test yourself in pursuit of the elusive perfect presentation.

While in college, I was always hesitant to present in front of the class. I just couldn't shake my nerves, but when I started my career and was given the opportunity to participate in new business presentations, I found a way to embrace the challenge and put my anxiety behind me.

As you begin your career, take every opportunity to speak in front of an audience. It doesn't matter who you are addressing, or what you are speaking about. Every set of eyes looking back at you and the look on their faces will tell you if you are connecting with them. When it's over, replay it in your head to see what you'd change and what you'd keep. Then refine your delivery to project the air of an articulate, confident job candidate or new account executive.

I encourage my students to schedule as many informational interviews as they can so they can expand their networks and get more comfortable presenting their brand narrative. Once you secure that first job, watch how others present and emulate their best qualities and incorporate those into your delivery. Your passionate quest to deliver the perfect presentation will drive you to always be better than your last speech.

MAKE YOUR MARK

You are human. You are never going to be satisfied with your presentations. But continuously learn from those experiences and apply the lessons learned to the next opportunity no matter how big or small the audience size.

LESSON 17

LISTEN MORE, SPEAK LESS

Listening is the most challenging – and underrated – skill in business. It takes a lot of discipline to fight the urge to constantly show what you know, but if you can commit to listening to the hiring professional's questions, you will deliver more thoughtful, effective answers. When you are assigned your first project, listen carefully and respond accurately.

Too often, I have witnessed executives not listen intently enough to their clients' requests and then struggle to explain why their verbal response or PowerPoint presentation doesn't match the request. That reminds me of a senior-level executive whom I admire. He will not say a word for 55 minutes of a 60-minute brainstorm or strategy session. Instead, he is actively listening to everyone's input, collecting and sorting data in real-time, so that he can deliver well-informed analysis and direction.

As you begin your career, prioritize listening and understand how that quality prepares you for bigger things.

MAKE YOUR MARK

There is a reason we have two ears and one mouth. With mentors, listen more than you speak; you are learning from them, not just showing them how smart you are, so make it easy for them to share their wisdom about life and business.

LESSON 18

EMBRACE DIVERSITY

You already know what you think. From the first day of your first internship and throughout your career, fully embrace diversity in order to open your mind to new ideas, opportunities and possibilities you never considered.

What does it mean to embrace diversity? It means being comfortable enough in your own skin to not think you have all the answers. Embrace diversity and put yourself in someone else's shoes and see how they, like you, are the product of their upbringing and experiences. It is through diverse ideation and problem solving that the greatest solutions will be developed in response to the most daunting business challenges.

MAKE YOUR MARK

You will often find yourself at a crossroads throughout your career. When you have two choices to make, take the one that will lead to collaboration with the individuals who represent the most diverse ideas, insights and innovative solutions for any project.

LESSON 19

CURIOSITY CREATES OPPORTUNITIES

My longtime business partner, Bryan Harris, preaches about the need for curiosity when he speaks to students and young executives. He believes it is essential to demonstrate curiosity especially during a job or internship interview.

From the moment you start an internship or a new job, ask questions. Why? I was hoping you would ask that...

People are eager to explain what they know and will see you as an employee interested in learning more about the company you work for and the job you do. Remember, too, that curiosity extends well beyond the workplace. Outside the office, be open to learning and experiencing new things. Become a voracious reader, consuming books and publications you never would have picked up before. Attend events that are out of your comfort zone and take a journey down a less traveled road; you will expand your horizons, meet new people and learn many new things that will influence your career.

MAKE YOUR MARK

If it ain't broke, break it. Okay, perhaps not literally, but curiosity leads to innovation and innovation leads to personal and career transformation.

LESSON 20

WORK HARD, BE NICE

My friend Sammy Steinlight, whom I referred to earlier, has spent most of his career working at Madison Square Garden and its various entities (New York Knicks, Rangers, Liberty). He regularly dealt with high-profile, high-intensity situations, managing the needs of members of the media and a vocal group of fans.

He covers a variety of topics each time he speaks to my public relations classes, but never fails to deliver one simple message. "Work hard and be nice," he says. Then he watches the students roll their eyes and think he's just another grown-up telling them what to do, until he reminds them that being kind is not the same as being soft or timid or a pushover. It does mean that, if you can keep calm while everyone else is going crazy, you will get things accomplished.

I am asked frequently why I have worked at Taylor for more than 25 years. My answer mirrors Steinlight's insight: Taylor has earned a reputation, creating an environment that puts a premium on working hard and being dedicated to excellence. We live and breathe a team-first mentality, a collaborative approach and treat every colleague with the utmost respect. If you can approach your internship or first job with that same mindset, you will be happy, highly productive and earn the respect and admiration of your colleagues and clients.

MAKE YOUR MARK

"Work hard and be nice" is more than a catchphrase. It's a philosophy you should embody throughout your career. Find the workplace that values those attributes.

LESSON 21

BE READY FOR ANYTHING

When my students ask for advice regarding their job search, I ask them to tell me what they are most passionate about. Then I let them know that, while not every project they work on will align with their passion, being open to new experiences will help them develop new passions.

When I graduated from college, all I wanted was a career in sports. Nearly 30 years later, I rarely work in sports, but I learned that my true passion was marketing itself. It doesn't matter what the product is, I love that research informs the strategic and creative approach to solving a business challenge. Quite often, your market research leads you in an unexpected direction. Instead of ruling it out because it doesn't match your initial plan, be prepared to follow where the new information leads. All of us, whether starting a career or decades into it, must be open-minded at all times to opportunities and experiences.

MAKE YOUR MARK

Be the executive who is least afraid of change and capable of pivoting at a moment's notice. That open-mindedness will lead to the start of the next exciting chapter in your career.

LESSON 22

HUSTLE OFTEN BEATS TALENT

"I look for someone with something to prove – to your old boss, your dad, your third-grade teacher, yourself. I don't care where it comes from: You need that hustle," said Emily Weiss, Founder and CEO of Glossier[3].

I coached all my children in youth sports and often used my favorite phrase – "It doesn't take ability to hustle" – on them and their teammates. You may be the least skilled player on the basketball court or the soccer pitch, but if you hustle, you can often beat more skilled opponents. That work ethic applies in the office, too.

Show that hustle to help you get the job or internship you want. It will differentiate you from the candidate with the higher GPA or more prestigious alma mater who oozes an air of entitlement. But be careful, this hustle doesn't need to make you look like a show-off. It means putting in extra effort to learn, finding a detail that helps your boss make his boss happy or helps close a deal. Hustle is the difference between an average colleague and a great one.

MAKE YOUR MARK

Hustle is evidence of a good work ethic and putting the project ahead of your pride. It's the difference between retaining a client and losing one at the end of the year. When you hustle, others will follow your lead.

---

3. "How Great Leaders Hire The Right People." (2017, January 9). Retrieved from https://www.fastcompany.com/3066364/work-smart/how-great-leaders-hire-the-right-people

LESSON 23

MAKE DREAMS COME TRUE

When I look into the eyes of my students and tell them their dreams of landing a certain job or working for a specific company or organization will come true, they are skeptical... at first. When I repeat that same message over an entire semester, they slowly become believers.

I have seen one of my college classmates, Mike Emanuel, go from covering local news in Midland, Texas, one of the smallest television markets in the nation, to working in the White House every day covering the President of the United States for a leading national cable network. As 20-year-old Rutgers University students, Mike and I called the football and basketball broadcasts for WRSU, the university radio station. It was clear that broadcasting was Mike's passion, and while covering the president every day might have just been a dream, he dedicated himself to make that dream a reality. He started small and kept refining his skills. He worked his way up, then he moved to a bigger market, then the next, before eventually getting his shot to reach a national news outlet with millions of viewers.

MAKE YOUR MARK

If you are lucky enough to find your calling early, pursue it and enjoy every step of the journey, confident that your dream will come true. If you aren't sure what your purpose is, keep trying new things until you find it.

LESSON 24

ANYTHING IS POSSIBLE

Less than three years after graduating from college, I was in Albertville, France, leading the sponsorship activation for a major consumer brand at the Olympic Games.

Sitting in a dorm room with my buddies during my last semester in college, I never imagined anything like that could happen. Heck, I still didn't have a job lined up. But I knew what I wanted to do, and kept pursuing every angle until I got that first job. When I look back at the global sports experience in 1992, I can draw a direct connection to my internship several years earlier prior to my senior year that ultimately led me to be in a position to seize an opportunity that I once considered impossible.

Anything – any job, responsibility or opportunity – is possible, but it is up to you to create your own breaks.

MAKE YOUR MARK

Develop a list of career-oriented aspirations that seem impossible to achieve right now. Keep that list handy as you evolve in your career. Don't be afraid to add to it – and work tirelessly to feel the sense of accomplishment that comes from crossing those pie-in-the-sky items off the list.

LESSON 25

BE HAPPY

Happy people are productive people, and vice versa. It may be a chicken-or-egg debate on which comes first, but one certainty is that happiness is contagious. If you can be that happy person in the office, you will be more productive and that will rub off on your peers.

It might seem silly, or obvious, or even shocking that leaving college for a life in the workforce can bring happiness. After all, it's called a job for a reason. But if you are going to be spending the next 40 years (sorry, didn't mean to scare you!) at work, you'd better find a way to make it enjoyable. You fought so hard to get your job, but that should never be the reason you stay with it. If you are miserable, work hard to find another one that will make you happy.

MAKE YOUR MARK

Here's another newsflash: You will spend more hours at work than in just about any part of your weekly life. Match your talents and passion with a corporate culture that satisfies both and you'll enjoy virtually every day on the job.

LESSON 26

BE FEARLESS

There are plenty of reasons to worry about your entry into the workforce. But you have nothing holding you back, so be bold!

If you want a job or internship, find out how you can get it on your own or who can help you find the right person to connect with. Exude unshakeable confidence and competence, the essential characteristics that those who are hiring graduates look for.

As the saying goes, you get one chance to make a first impression – and there are a lot of other college graduates who want that job, too. Be fearless in your approach and the possibilities are limitless.

MAKE YOUR MARK

Don't be afraid to leave to get what you want. You don't have a mortgage, a spouse or a child. If you get the chance to move anywhere to take advantage of an opportunity you'd never get at home, go for it!

LESSON 27

LEAN ON OTHERS

You may be just at the starting line of your career marathon, but you never have to run alone.

In my experience at Taylor, I am most inspired by the way we lean on each other to solve the business challenges that our clients face. Collaborative teams that build on each other's ideas and concepts develop the most strategic and creative solutions to business challenges.

Aside from your handpicked mentors, continuously develop your own collaborative team to lean on for counsel, advice and a favor or two.

MAKE YOUR MARK

You are capable of achieving great things on your own, but don't be fooled into thinking that it can't be enhanced with the support of others. Lean on your personal and professional networks and you will achieve what once you may have considered impossible.

LESSON 28

THINK LIKE AN ENTREPRENEUR

From the moment you begin to network and apply for internships and jobs, start thinking like an entrepreneur. And when you earn that job you've worked so hard on, bring that mindset with you. Don't follow the status quo. Create your own path to success. That could mean taking an entirely new approach to creating your traditional resumé or making strategic recommendations as an intern based on your social-media prowess.

While entrepreneurs are typically applauded for starting innovative companies and leading them to success, each of us has an entrepreneurial spirit. You just need to unlock it and apply it to your career development.

MAKE YOUR MARK

Remember that your first job gets you in the front door. Once you are in, find the departments and colleagues known for their entrepreneurial instincts and find a way to work with them.

LESSON 29:

OBSERVE OTHERS

Once you find a job or internship, there will be plenty to learn.

Keep your eyes and ears open for clues – good or bad – that can unlock your potential to grow in the company. You will find yourself in situations that you've likely never experienced before, so be a sponge. When you are in a meeting, observe how the most effective executives articulate their points-of-view and earn respect while other executives spend their time staring at their laptops answering emails or socializing with friends outside the office.

Develop your "EQ," or emotional intelligence, to inform the way that you should, and shouldn't, do business.

MAKE YOUR MARK

I know that it is the single-most important thing to a 22-year-old (and many others, too), but put the smartphone away. Think nobody caught you scrolling through Snapchat during that operations meeting? Think again.

LESSON 30

PROCEED WITH PURPOSE

As a new employee, focus on making an impact with everything that you do. You don't have the luxury of taking a minute, an hour, an afternoon off, so have purpose in every task you perform or every meeting you sit in.

It amazes me when I see a young executive spend 60 minutes in a meeting just taking up space with no intent or purpose. Determine what your primary objective is in every work interaction; take notes, write down terms you don't know, make sure you clearly understand everything that is being asked of you.

MAKE YOUR MARK

Other than your reputation, time is one of your most valuable assets. Proceed with purpose throughout your career and your time will be well invested.

LESSON 31

EXERCISE YOUR BODY, FREE YOUR MIND

I attribute much of my career success and longevity to 30 years of exercise. I skied in my 20s, ran marathons in my 30s, cycled in my 40s and now spend more time swimming.

Whether I am trying to solve a business challenge or create the "next big idea," engaging my body allows my brain to run free. Somewhere during the course of my workout, an idea pops into my head. Then I go on physical autopilot while I work through the details. I return home, type it out and send it to my colleagues before 8 a.m.

Exercise will leave you feeling energized and motivated to take on all challenges and create new opportunities at work.

MAKE YOUR MARK

Your passion might be a team sport like basketball or soccer or a singular pursuit like yoga or kickboxing. Either way, find balance with exercise to stay active and channel that feeling like a little kid playing after school.

LESSON 32

ESTABLISH YOUR METRICS FOR SUCCESS

In business, every initiative is evaluated by pre-determined metrics for success. As you begin your transition from student to employee, identify your metrics for progress.

As a student, a metric for success may include networking with a specific number of executives and influencers in your industry of choice before your junior or senior year. As you approach graduation, a metric may be to exceed a certain number of informational interviews before you receive your diploma.

Establish your unique set of metrics for success to define your early career goals and the timeline you believe it will take to achieve them. Achieving milestones will provide you the benchmarks you will need to evaluate the success of your efforts as you begin your career.

MAKE YOUR MARK

"If you don't know where you're going, any road will take you there." This old saying was born before metrics were invented, but message is the same: Make the plan. Work the plan. Adjust the plan.

PART II

PREPARING FOR YOUR CAREER AFTER COLLEGE

LESSON 33

DEMONSTRATE A SENSE OF URGENCY

I will go out of my way to help any student or young executive who demonstrates a sense of urgency about their career. However, there is nothing more damaging than a young executive not responding in a timely manner when they receive assistance from a mentor or someone in their network.

I can recall every time I have leveraged my professional network and arranged a meeting via an email introduction for a student or young executive with a well-established professional in a specific industry and they did not immediately respond and arrange a day and time for the call or meeting. Instead, days ago by before the student eventually joins the conversation.

Never wait for more than a minute when someone offers career assistance. Be highly responsive and jump on every opportunity that is presented to you. Continue that timely approach when you start your internship or first job and make it a habit for the rest of your career. In this case, good things will come to those who don't wait. The window could close on opportunities for you with every minute you wait to respond.

MAKE YOUR MARK

John Wooden, a legendary basketball coach at UCLA, finished every pregame speech with this piece of advice: "Go fast, but never hurry." Translation: Do it quickly, but make sure it's right.

LESSON 34

ERROR FREE WORK WILL EXPEDITE YOUR JOURNEY

A longtime friend, Vincent Mallozzi, is a journalist and author. He tells my students that if a publicist misspells his name in a pitch for a story, he pitches it right back – into the trash.

It doesn't matter what business you are in, error-free communication is mandatory. Whether it is an email, a creative brief, a business proposal or a thank-you note, a single error in your writing is unacceptable. You would be surprised how may resumés I have reviewed that include misspellings. Once someone in Human Resources catches an error in your resumé or cover letter, your written application will go right into the shredder.

MAKE YOUR MARK

Commit to a zero-tolerance policy when it comes to errors in your writing. Before you submit any correspondence, have someone with a fresh set of eyes proofread your document.

LESSON 35

EXPERIENCE COUNTS

It used to surprise me when a student submitted a resumé to me that listed no experience. Now I realize that it is a trend, and my surprise has turned to disappointment.

When I interview candidates, I don't ask about the school they attended or what their GPA was. Instead, I focus solely on the work experiences they had in college, because it shows me that the applicant could juggle the demands of managing course work, part-time jobs and any other extracurricular activities they participated in.

A recent graduate, Kristina Amaral, who has served as a guest lecturer in my classes, shares with students her story: She is a theater buff with a passion for marketing, so she walked into the offices of a local theater company and volunteered to support their social-media marketing efforts. It was her first experience for her resumé, but she used it in her interviews to demonstrate the initiative that she showed to get experience in anticipation of getting a job.

You can never have too much experience. It's one of the reasons that Eric Liebler, president of ProCamps Worldwide, annually offers one-day experiences in event management and sports marketing to hundreds of college students nationwide. Once you get your first taste of experience – any kind of experience – then start pursuing work experience that is relevant to the industry you would like to find a fulltime job in. Along the way, expand your professional network any time you can.

MAKE YOUR MARK

If you have already graduated and don't have any experience, you might benefit by taking an internship position. Once you show what you are capable of, you might be able to parlay the experience into a full-time opportunity.

LESSON 36

YOUR RESUMÉ WILL NEVER BE PERFECT

While I have always reviewed resumés as part of my role with my public relations agency, it wasn't until I started teaching that I began reviewing a high volume of original resumés, as well as second and third drafts, as well as helping students develop one-page "sell sheets." I could dedicate an entire book to resumé development, but for now I will provide some helpful tips based on the hundreds I have reviewed over the past several years:

- Feature relevant experience and accomplishments

- Ensure there are no typos

- Include your contact information

- Use black type

- Use a slightly larger font for your name; it is your brand and needs to stand out

- Don't list every course you ever took

- Be consistent; include three bullets points to detail each experience

- Begin each bullet point with an action verb

- Never use a period at the end of a bullet point

- Highlight your social and digital-media skills

- Ensure consistent spacing and design (bold, underline, italics and punctuation)

- Creative types can use non-traditional designs, as long as they are not distracting
- Ensure your resumé looks professional and well organized
- Update regularly with new experiences and accomplishments

MAKE YOUR MARK

Did I mention that you should check for typos?

LESSON 37

CUT TO THE POINT WITH YOUR COVER LETTER

I review hundreds of cover letters for my students. And virtually every one of them shows that students treat a cover letter like a narrative resume. This is not a letter to a long-lost friend. It's a quick introduction to prove your value to the company.

Your resumé provides your work history and credentials, and it's attached to your cover letter, so all you need to craft is an efficient, effective three-paragraph cover letter.

Open with a paragraph that explains your interest in the company and the exact title of the position you are applying for. In your second paragraph, feature a few personal and professional highlights. Then conclude your letter with a paragraph thanking the hiring manager for their consideration. Get in, get out, then wait for the call to come in for the interview!

MAKE YOUR MARK

A survey of hiring managers reported that 90 percent of them read cover letters, BUT 100 percent of them say you have 10 seconds to make an impression. Get to the point, make it count.

LESSON 38

YOUR FRIENDS TODAY ARE TOMORROW'S DECISION MAKERS

It may be hard to fathom but that guy you teamed up with in beer pong last night or the sorority sister you met at a tailgate party before a football game that neither of you actually attended, will eventually be C-suite executives, company founders and individuals of influence.

When I think back to my friends and acquaintances from college, I am amazed at just how much talent was assembled on campus. More than 25 years after graduation, another of my former college radio partners, Gordon Deal, hosts a national morning radio show on hundreds of stations. As mentioned earlier, Mike Emanuel covers politics for a popular national cable television network and another is a senior producer for a top-rated national morning show on one of the major television networks.

The lesson here? Start networking at parties… honestly, the friendships you make in college could prove to be mutually beneficial as you all climb the corporate ladder. You have already done the hard work and established friendships and mutual respect. Now, nurture those relationships as you begin your career. If I have a regret looking back more than 25 years, it is that I did not maintain communication with more of the young men and women with whom I spent four years in class and other social activities.

MAKE YOUR MARK

Each and every individual you attend class with can become foundational members of your professional network and running partners on your 30-year career marathon.

LESSON 39

PURSUE YOUR PASSION

Sometimes your career path is right in front of you... A world-class track athlete from one of the nation's most decorated universities sought my advice. She'd earned her degree in communications, but was so focused on her track career that she wasn't prepared for it all to end and had no idea where to "run" next. To me, it was simple; she just had to follow her passion. I told her there were hundreds of jobs in running and communications or marketing with footwear and athletic-apparel manufacturers, event marketers and media companies. She had never even considered that a career option.

Of course, it was the same basic philosophy I share with all young people: Whether it is music, movies, sports, travel, food or fashion, there are careers for every passion point, I believe the most logical path to pursue comes when your passion intersects with the focus of your studies. Why? Your passion point is something that you should be incredibly knowledgeable about and something that you would enjoy working on for the next 30 or more years.

MAKE YOUR MARK

Confucius wrote, "Choose a job you love and you will never work a day in your life."

LESSON 40

BECOME A CATEGORY EXPERT

If you pursue your passion, whatever that might be, become an expert in it. If you are early in your college career and reading this book, use this advice to get a head start on your peers.

The explosion of social media gives anyone who invests the time, energy and focus, the opportunity to turn themselves into a category expert.

How? Let's say your goal is to land a career in the music business. The first step is to launch a Twitter handle specifically dedicated to music news and content. Then you need to actively and frequently post and share relevant, compelling content. Simultaneously, start your own music blog providing analysis, opinion and expert reporting. Post often, then amplify your content via dedicated Facebook, Instagram and YouTube channels. As you gain followers and credibility, seek out interview opportunities with bands and record labels – and don't ignore the promoters and brands who play a critical role in the industry.

MAKE YOUR MARK

Find your passion point, analyze the market and find a way to turn yourself into a category expert that will easily differentiate yourself from all other candidates seeking a position in your chosen category.

LESSON 41

MAKE YOUR WAY INTO THE INNER CIRCLE

If you pursue your passion and become a category expert, now you need to find your way into the inner circle.

I believe that each industry – music, fashion, food, sports, finance – is part of a business solar system, each represented by a giant circle. Often, these circles intersect, as with sports and music. If your primary objective is to work in the music industry, you need to determine how to get inside the circle, because once you do, the possibilities are endless. Accessing the circle may be highly challenging, but that is where professional networking, informational interviews and industry experience are essential building blocks.

For example, if one of my students asked me how they could access the music circle, my first call would be to Jon Landman, founder of The Syndicate, a music and entertainment marketing agency based in Weehawken, NJ. Jon is always looking to give students a break into the music industry. When a student gains access into the circle, I congratulate them and inform them that now they need to make the most of the opportunity because "cracking the code" is just the first step – and if you don't deliver, you will find yourself back outside the circle.

MAKE YOUR MARK

Everybody wants a seat at the table, but once you get there, you have to let them know you belong. When the opportunity comes, have the ideas ready to go and the desire to bring the idea to life.

LESSON 42

RESEARCH AND RECRUIT YOUR FUTURE EMPLOYER

Just as universities scout and recruit accomplished athletes for their teams, you can apply the same principles to finding the perfect employer.

First, identify brands and organizations that you are passionate about and industries that excite you and add them to your target list. Once you have identified the targets, conduct extensive research regarding culture, turnover rates and any other information that will help you find a way into their organization.

Once you've done the legwork, do a crosscheck of your personal and professional networks to see if they can help you arrange a "recruiting trip," the same way you visited colleges and universities while you were in high school. This plan of action allows you to take control of your prospecting efforts.

If you are fortunate enough to be able to "walk the halls," you will then be well informed to make the decision if you want to officially throw your hat in the ring for the opportunity to formally interview for a position with your potential future employer. This proactive and strategic approach flips the way most students and graduates take in securing their first job.

MAKE YOUR MARK

As the lyrics to a song by country-music legend Randy Travis go, "Since the phone still ain't ringin'/I assume it still ain't you..." Take control of your job search by making it impossible for them to ignore you. Shown them who you are and why they need to hire you.

LESSON 43

BE CULTURALLY RELEVANT

My daughter, a junior in college at the time I was writing this book, received a course assignment to attend a performance by a jazz ensemble. When she returned, she said, "That was an eye-opening and interesting new experience." Without knowing it, she was becoming culturally relevant.

As you prepare to graduate and begin your career, become more culturally relevant and take time to visit a museum, attend an opera, see a musical at a community theater and listen to a poetry reading.

It will jumpstart your transformation from a student to a professional. It will also break you out of your four-year routine of classes, studying and partying. Most importantly, it will introduce you to new experiences that you can socialize via job interviews, conversations with co-workers and networking meetings with professionals you admire.

MAKE YOUR MARK

The workplace is not like college. You will deal with people of all ages, backgrounds and interests. You will stand out among your peers when you can talk to anyone about anything. Like my daughter, you might discover that you love some of these cultural experiences and, in the process, uncover a new passion point.

LESSON 44

GET OUT OF YOUR COMFORT ZONE

In becoming more culturally relevant, you are forcing yourself to get out of your comfort zone. When I was in college, my world rotated around my classes in journalism and broadcasting and my passion for sports, which led me to either attend many athletic events or broadcast them on the student radio station.

That was great as a student, but it was not going to cut it when I made the jump into the real world. Nearly 30 years after graduating from college, I still force myself to get out of my comfort zone, whether that means taking dance lessons or going back to school to earn my master's degree before I turned 50.

At first, I was uncomfortable in each of those situations, but ultimately it led to new experiences that ignited my creativity and zest for life, in and away from the office.

MAKE YOUR MARK

Know who you are, then do everything you can to shake yourself out of your comfort zone. It will open up an entirely new world to you, which will help you evolve as an individual and a professional. You will be very glad you did.

LESSON 45

MEET INTERESTING PEOPLE

Aside from your professional networking efforts, starting a new job means you will be leaving your college cocoon and have to be open to meeting a whole new cast of characters – co-workers, bosses, clients, new roommate, the guy at the dry cleaner, the woman who owns the sandwich shop near the office – and you must learn how to connect with all of them.

This kind of change can be overwhelming, unless you appreciate the inspiration it can bring. When you were a college freshman, you had to remove your blinders, explore a whole new world and find a way to fit in. Now, as a new professional, you are a freshman all over again. It is time to shift your worldview again and be open to meeting new people who challenge what you think you know.

I have been fascinated by the recent increase in individuals who identify themselves as motivational speakers. One in particular is Mike Pierce, who goes by "Antarctic Mike." He travels the world delivering motivational speeches to corporations and organizations. His claim to fame is that he is one of the first nine people to run the first Antarctic Ice Marathon. He followed that up by returning to compete in the Antarctic Ultra Marathon, a 62.1-mile run in sub-zero temperatures.

I am fascinated that Mike has made a career out of booking speaking engagements nearly every day of the year, inspiring thousands of people with his message: "Extreme Conditions…Extraordinary Results." He's just one interesting individual whom I have gone out of my way to meet and build a relationship with. He inspires me every time we have a conversation and I leave those discussions with dozens of creative ideas.

MAKE YOUR MARK

Whether it's meeting an interesting person who runs marathons in the Antarctic or someone who moonlights as an improvisational comedian, seek out people who do something you'd never consider trying and see if it sparks your creativity.

LESSON 46

TRY SOMETHING FOR THE FIRST TIME

A few times during presentations, I have asked C-suite executives, "When was the last time you did something for the first time?" I was then met with silence, followed by inquisitive looks. So I ask it again, until I see heads start to nod.

We all get into routines and forget what it is like to experience something new. Think back to when you got your first job and your first paycheck, drove a car for the first time or packed the car to leave for college for the first time. Each experience might have made you a little nervous, but you fought through the anxiety to start a new journey.

So, here you are again, getting ready to take on new responsibilities at work, support a community organization or join a professional networking club. It does not matter what it is. The key is to consistently try new things and in the process expose yourself to new challenges, experiences and people who will help you evolve professionally and personally.

MAKE YOUR MARK

Your parents didn't let you get away with saying you didn't like something that you had never tried. Now that you are on your own, don't let yourself off the hook. Go for it!

LESSON 47

FACE YOUR FEARS

In offering advice to college students in an article in Inc., billionaire Warren Buffett said how he was "petrified" to speak in public and decided to face his fears head on. He recounts how he saw an advertisement on public speaking in a newspaper. "I gave the guy $100 in cash. It changed my life[4]." (4)

Like Buffett, many students have a fear of speaking in public, going on a job interview or even attending a social function and attempting to make small talk. That is no way to live, so face your fears and beat them, just as Buffett did.

I can relate. As a high school student, I got incredibly nervous each time I had to present in a class. I can't remember the precise moment that I conquered that fear, but I knew that I would never succeed in marketing until I could be comfortable in front of crowds.

To this day, my heart beats fast every time I present but I channel that nervousness into confidence and passion when I am front of an audience and it has worked. I have stood before senior executives from many Fortune 500 companies and have been on the winning side of competitive agency pitches. If I had not faced my fear, I would have lost every time.

MAKE YOUR MARK

"The brave man is not he who does not feel afraid," Nelson Mandela said, "but he who conquers that fear."

---

4. Hwang, Y. L. (2017, January 30). Bill Gates' and Warren Buffett's Top Advice for College Students. Retrieved from http://www. inc.com/yeho-lucy-hwang/warren-buffett-to-college-students-curiosity-can-change-your-life.html

LESSON 48

THE LITTLE THINGS COUNT

While your sights may be set on networking with senior-level decision makers or getting the "big job" with a large corporation, none of them will happen unless you believe that the little things count every step of the way.

From each detail in your resumé to every word in a cover letter or thank-you note, sweat the small stuff.

Ultimately, you may secure that job you were coveting or that meeting with a C-suite executive, but it is a combination of many small steps and actions that will lead you to achieving your objectives. There are no short cuts. Delve into every detail of networking, applying for a position and securing internships and relevant experience.

Every time I prepare for a presentation, I methodically research every individual whom I anticipate meeting. I want to learn where they attended college, what their previous experience is and how they spend their free time. This approach to uncovering the little things about individuals demonstrates an attention to detail that will resonate with the audience and set you apart from the competition.

MAKE YOUR MARK

Whether you are writing, presenting or leading a discussion, you will be more comfortable if you have done your homework. The more comfortable you feel, the more likely you are to close the deal.

LESSON 49

KNOW 10 TOPICS YOU CAN DISCUSS FOR 10 MINUTES

Whether at work, a networking event or a social function, it is vital to master the art of making conversation.

Longtime public relations practitioner David Siroty, whom I referenced earlier in the book, is a big believer in being completely conversant in 10 topics across various segments – sports, pop culture, politics, music, food, movies, business, to name a few - that you can discuss for 10 minute each. It's what makes Dave one of those people who draws a crowd at functions. He has the ability to carry on a conversation with anyone across a variety of topics.

If your 10 topics are your secret weapon, you can pivot and transition off of any conversation that you walk into and spin the conversation into one of your areas of expertise. Applying this lesson also extends your ability to converse with a diverse group of people, regardless of age, gender or background.

This lesson came to life when one of my students participated in a two-day job interview with a leading online retailer. Upon arrival, the first test was to attend a welcome function, where the employer was observing if the candidates could carry on conversations for 60 minutes or if they shied away from mixing with the other attendees.

MAKE YOUR MARK

It's easy to earn the wrong reputation very quickly, so master the 10-topics-in-10-minutes lesson and you will always be at the center of the conversation.

PART III

INSIGHTS FOR INTERVIEWING

LESSON 50

INFORMATIONAL INTERVIEWS MAKE FOR A GREAT DRESS REHEARSAL

Many students are dismissive of landing an "informational interview," when companies grant time to meet and screen individuals, even if there is no present job openings.

"It's only an informational interview," they say, as though they don't need to take it too seriously. Informational interviews are incredibly valuable and you should schedule as many as you can. Just about any executive will take the time to meet with a student or graduate especially if the meeting is labeled an "informational interview." One of my first informational interviews was at ABC News where I ended up sitting for several hours in a very busy newsroom as news was breaking. That was exciting.

Treat informational interviews as dress rehearsals for formal interviews in the future. From the research you conduct and the questions you prepare, to the way you dress and the manner in which you make the strongest possible first impression, informational interviews can serve as your off-Broadway performance before you make it to the big time. It not only serves as a chance to rehearse, but you are expanding your network in the process and don't be surprised if you receive a call back.

MAKE YOUR MARK

If you make the right impression with that executive across the desk, they will most likely consider you for a future opening at their organization.

LESSON 51

ARTICULATE YOUR ATTITUDE

More and more students and graduates are conducting their first interview by phone as part of a screening process. When you agree to this, you are likely getting into a long process that will involve multiple rounds of evaluation.

My students frequently ask me how they should conduct a phone interview. Unless you are on Skype or FaceTime, the person conducting the interview can't see you, your body language or your facial expressions. They will base their judgment on whether you will earn the right to make it to the next round primarily on your voice and the way you shape your narrative. The rest of my advice is simple:

- Call from a landline, not your cell phone.

- Find a very quiet room with no noise or distractions; it will allow you to stay focused. You don't want to be conducting this call from the recreation room of the fraternity or sorority house.

- Speak with confidence and volume. If you conduct the call at a low volume and exude shyness, you will never advance to the next round. Your confidence must come through the phone line in order to earn a call back.

MAKE YOUR MARK

No: "Umm," "Yup," "Know what I'm sayin'" or "I mean…" Yes: "Thank you for your time," "Yes, I agree…," "I am most comfortable when…" and "It's been a pleasure to speak with you…"

LESSON 52

SCRIPT YOUR SKYPE SESSION

Congratulations, you made it to the second round, also known as the Skype session. Like the phone interview, you need to prepare properly and focus on additional elements that were not relevant to a phone call.

With an interview by Skype or some form of streaming video, the interviewer can now see you and can make judgments based on your body language, facial expressions, the way you dress and even your physical surroundings.

Like a phone interview, my advice is simple. First, give thought to the exact location where you plan to conduct the interview and ensure there is nothing unusual in the background that will distract the interviewer. In other words, don't conduct this interview in your dormitory when your roommates are just getting into week-end party mode. Secondly, be thoughtful about what you will be wearing. Again, it will be a factor that could be the difference between advancing to the next round or not.

MAKE YOUR MARK

No raunchy posters or unmade beds in the background. In the foreground, dress professionally, be confident and sit up straight – and do a dry run to ensure that your phone line or network can handle the call.

LESSON 53

BE CONFIDENT, NOT COCKY, WHEN INTERVIEWING

When my students ask me to help them prepare for a job interview, one of the messages I always communicate no matter the student is, "to be confident, not cocky" when interviewing. When interviewing for a potential position, the interviewer is taking everything into consideration, so present yourself as a young professional. Make eye contact when you meet the interviewer, reach out your hand and offer a firm, confident handshake. Greet them by their first name, thank them for the time and the opportunity to meet.

I have conducted far too many interviews where the job candidate offered me the "dead fish" handshake, a half-hearted offering of their hand. No energy, no commitment, no confidence... and no job. Sometimes, that is all is takes to identify the wrong candidate.

MAKE YOUR MARK

If you can't get past the handshake, how are you going to instill confidence that you are passionate about getting the job? Practice a firm (not bone-crushing) handshake, look the person in the eye, then knock the interview out of the park by sitting up straight, being an active listener and confidently articulating each and every response.

LESSON 54

DRESS THE PART

One of the most frequent questions I get asked before a student or graduate conducts a job interview is, "What should I wear?"

While it seems like a simple ask, it is actually very important. Before you visit any organization, ask and learn what the appropriate way to dress is as the rules of fashion in the workplace have changed significantly over the past several years. If you are meeting with investment firms on Wall Street, a suit and tie may be the best choice, while an interview with a social media or advertising agency might only require blue jeans, a button-down shirts and sneakers.

Dress codes are fluid these days, so you have to be prepared for anything. I recall a story of an agency team that showed up for a meeting with an action-sports company in suits and ties. One team member is sure they lost the account the minute they walked in. They were overdressed and didn't look like they had done their homework on the company's corporate and cultural vibe. The bottom line is to be proactive and ask your point-of-contact at the company how you should dress for the interview.

MAKE YOUR MARK

You can always take off a tie, or put one on, before a meeting. If you aren't sure, arrive early and see how the employees look as they arrive for work.

LESSON 55

INTERVIEW EMPLOYERS

When you finally get the call for a job interview, shift your mindset and think about how you are going to interview your potential employer.

Too often, students and graduates focus solely on the types of questions they are going to be asked and how they are going to answer them. The secret to a successful interview is to turn it into a conversation. The way to do that is to develop smart questions.

You want to avoid feeling like you just sweated through an interrogation and instead, enjoy a substantive conversation. Everyone takes pride in speaking about themselves, their organization and their project and campaign experience. The key is you need to ask the interviewer those types of personal and professional questions in a way that naturally elevates the interview into a conversation.

MAKE YOUR MARK

Always research as much as possible about the individuals who are interviewing you and the organization itself. And, the day of the interview, scour appropriate industry sites and business publications to make sure no news broke overnight that could affect the tone of the interview.

LESSON 56

CULTURE IS CRITICALLY IMPORTANT

In a 400-level organizational leadership course I teach to graduating seniors, we dedicate an extraordinary amount of time to understanding what kind of corporate culture they think will give them the best opportunity to succeed. No two corporate cultures are the same, since each company's persona is determined by a variety of elements, including the management team, the people they hire and the organization's history, rituals and unspoken language. You not only need to uncover the culture of an organization during your interview process, but you need to determine the best culture for you. Ask yourself these questions:

- Do you excel in an environment where they take a laissez faire or country-club approach or would you prefer a more structured organization where hard work and long hours and even weekend duty is rewarded?

- Will you perform better in an atmosphere that is highly social and colleagues prioritize outings and events inside and outside the office or do you lean toward an environment where the exclusive focus is the task at hand and socializing is not important to you?

Once you determine the type of culture where you believe you will thrive, you then need to target an organization for employment that can deliver that cultural experience to you.

MAKE YOUR MARK

Once you identify the type of culture you'd like to join and what it's like in the company where you will interview, take nothing for granted. You are never really sure what it's like until you walk the halls. Pay attention as you make the interview rounds and uncover the culture on your own.

LESSON 57

USE SOCIAL MEDIA TO YOUR ADVANTAGE

When I tell students that their social-media skills are strong assets, they look at me with an inquisitive look. Yes, your knowledge and experience with social media is something that you should fully leverage before, during and after the job interview process. Think about it. You are fluent in social-media platforms, many of which you have been using for half of your lives. But that was for fun, now it's business.

As you get more serious about your career pursuit, use these channels to regularly share relevant content about your area of interest. During the interview process, determine how to integrate your experience with social channels into your personal narrative. When you finally start that first job, apply all the success you have had in driving social-media engagement for your personal channels and now use it to suit your business needs or help identify challenges for your company or the clients you counsel.

MAKE YOUR MARK

If you haven't gotten the job yet, behave on social media. Remember, if you're looking at them, what makes you think they aren't checking you out, too?

LESSON 58

HANDWRITTEN THANK YOU NOTES GET NOTICED

You have worked hard to meet people. When you have met them, you made the commitment to nurture the relationship. Now, do one simple thing that will have you standing out from the competition: send a handwritten thank-you note.

No, I am not joking… In a world dominated by texting and templated email correspondence, invest in branded thank-you cards and write a personal note to the individual who took the time to meet you and share their insights, lessons and recommendations. Then send it within a day of your meeting.

When you write your note, personalize it based on the topics you discussed in the meeting so that the recipient knows you actively listened. If they discussed a vacation they are taking or their favorite sports team, refer to it in your note. Believe it or not, your thank-you note will last well beyond an email "thank you." The recipient will not only be pleasantly surprised, they will socialize it and walk the halls and share with colleagues. It is a very simple approach to break through the clutter and stand out among a crowded field of students and graduates.

MAKE YOUR MARK

Showing that you have some "old school" swagger in your game is a way of showing that you know how some aspects of business get done.

LESSON 59

BE PERSISTENT AND PROACTIVE IN YOUR FOLLOW-UP

You worked hard to get the interview, so why wouldn't you work just as hard after the interview? For every interview you go on, you should have a strategic timeline to guide your follow-up: After writing and sending a thank-you note as highlighted in the previous lesson, you should send a smart email within the next week. Use that email to reference a news story or some other conversational topic that is relevant to your conversation.

You should continue your follow-up every few weeks to maintain contact and provide updates. If the interview was regarding a specific internship or position, then you will want to be direct in your follow-up in determining your status for the potential opportunity.

MAKE YOUR MARK

If you waited more than two weeks to communicate with the person who interviewed you, the initial meeting or interview was a waste of your time as you did not have a persistent and proactive follow-up plan.

LESSON 60

SOMETIMES, THE WAITING IS THE SMARTEST PART

Too often, I hear my students concerned that it is only a few weeks after graduation and they don't have their first job yet. I try to calm their anxieties and let them know, the job will come. They just need to be patient while being proactive in their search. Often, waiting for the right opportunity is much better than jumping at the first job you are offered.

As I have written more than once in this book, success is a marathon. You are going to be invested in your career for the next several decades. Right now, you are only at the start line of that marathon – pace yourself. It's a long journey to the finish line. While some of your classmates may have gotten out to a fast start, there is plenty of time to catch up. Be less concerned about your peers and focus on the opportunity that is the best one for you.

MAKE YOUR MARK

There is no right or wrong here. If a job isn't waiting for you when you put on your cap and gown, control what you can control. Keep pitching and find a part-time job, internship or volunteer work to keep you busy as you continue your job search.

LESSON 61

PREPARE FOR PLAN B

Before I graduated from college, I had my heart set on a career as a sports broadcaster. It's what I did for most of my four years in school. I even interned at one of the largest radio stations in the nation and helped produce one of the first-ever major-market sports radio shows.

But it just didn't work out. I was fortunate that my Plan B was to pursue a career in public relations, because nearly 30 years later, I wouldn't change one thing about my career path. While you may be focused on a specific industry, organization or position, have a Plan B as part of your strategic approach to launching your career.

MAKE YOUR MARK

Plan B is not a second-place finish. Plan B is giving yourself more options and opportunities to pursue a career and secure that first job after you graduate.

PART IV

LEARNING ON THE JOB AND INTERNSHIP

LESSON 62

LOVE WHERE YOU ARE WORKING

I credit this lesson to one of my former students, David Pangilinan, who told me, "When you stop worrying about the next step in your career and focus on where you are working and the journey you took to get there, you become more productive and love what you are doing."

I completely agree with David. Once you secure that first full-time job, love everything about it – the challenges that you and your team solve each day, the people you collaborate with and the culture you are immersing yourself in.

Love is contagious. When you love your work, it inspires and empowers others around you. A positive attitude can only make others more positive.

MAKE YOUR MARK

From your first day on the job until the day you leave that organization, remind yourself to bring a positive mindset and approach to the office. Great things will follow.

LESSON 63

WALK AROUND AND MEET PEOPLE

Once you get that first internship or job, do not lock yourself in your cubicle and become hypnotized by your cell phone every time you get a break from your work. Instead, do something that very few people do today – stand up, take a walk around and introduce yourself to your colleagues. It will set you apart from your peers and open doors to new relationships, opportunities and experiences.

In today's corporate culture, too many young executives are satisfied with simply sitting at their desk, getting their work done and occasionally checking their phones to glance at any text messages and updates on their social-media channels. Your phone can wait until you are out of the office or at home later in the evening. Building relationships and establishing camaraderie with co-workers begins in the office setting and is critically important to your growth.

MAKE YOUR MARK

Building relationships in the office will pay dividends for many years to come as your career evolves.

LESSON 64

GET TO KNOW YOUR WORK FAMILY

Hard as it is to believe, you will spend more time with your work family than your actual family. Jonathan Neman, co-founder of Sweetgreen, commented in Fast Company, "People don't work for companies, they work for people. We don't have company meetings – we have family meetings[5]."

Neman is right, so take time to get to know your co-workers. Learn about their families, their passions and how they spend their time out of the office. Of course, there is a balancing act when it comes to work and socializing, but we shouldn't act like robots. If you are working alongside colleagues, you should be able to have discussions about life outside work. Your colleagues will take notice when you show genuine interest in their lives outside the workplace.

It can be as simple as knowing the name of their significant other and asking how he or she is doing or asking how their children are doing in in sports or other activities.

MAKE YOUR MARK

Take a few minutes every day to better understand what is in the hearts and mind of your colleagues and show interest in their lives. It will only lead to a more productive relationship with your work family.

---

5. Lessons In Leadership. (2017, February), Fast Company, (212), 22-23.

LESSON 65

GET FACE-TO-FACE MORE FREQUENTLY

Fast Company captured this lesson best when they wrote, "The reach you get from using Twitter, Facebook, Snapchat, Instagram – it's awesome. But reach is not the same thing as impact. To really connect, more often than not, we have to get face-to-face[6]."

There is no better way to make progress and be productive than to meet face-to-face and talk through an opportunity or challenge. Too many individuals who grew up on social media rely too much on text, instant message and email to communicate when a face-to-face meeting can be so much more impactful.

If you want to stand out from your peers, request face-to-face meetings with your managers and colleagues. It will be a pleasant surprise for those on the receiving end of your request as fewer executives ask for in-person meetings. Equally important, in most cases, it will be a more efficient and effective way to communicate.

MAKE YOUR MARK

It might be hard for you to do, but replace an ongoing text or email exchange with a 10-minute meeting over a cup of coffee. You will get to a solution quicker, get to know your colleague and set a new tone for your relationship.

---

6. Safian, R. (2017, February 1). How To Lead In 2017. Fast Company, 212, 12-13.

LESSON 66

LUNCH AND LEARN

Building on the impact of face-to-face meetings, take it one step further and schedule a lunch or breakfast meeting with a colleague you would like to get to know better or learn from. We all have to eat at some point during the day, so why not get out of your cubicle or office and discuss business while breaking bread.

Meeting over a meal can lead to quality time, especially if both of you turn off your mobile devices. It also creates an opportunity to go beyond business to establish a more personal connection, which is critical in evolving and building your relationship with someone you have identified as an influencer in your career development.

Participating in shared experiences like breakfast, lunch or dinner or going to a concert or a sports event with a colleague, mentor or person of influence is making an investment in your career and professional network. This type of investment in face-to-face quality time will pay dividends in the short and long term and contribute to your professional growth.

MAKE YOUR MARK

When you let down your guard and get to know colleagues on a personal level, it creates a connection that makes it easy to go the extra mile for them at work.

LESSON 67

BE SOCIAL

When it comes to "being social," I am not encouraging you to become more active with your social media channels. I am encouraging you to socialize the way executives did before social media and mobile phones were invented. While working hard and dedicating long hours is essential to career growth and advancement, so is socializing.

From playing on the company softball team to participating in a community-driven cause-related event that your employer supports, participate in each and every opportunity.

Once you have seamlessly integrated your company's social outings into your calendar, take it one step further and attend industry or young executive networking socials where you can extend your personal brand outside your office boundaries.

MAKE YOUR MARK

No, you are not too cool for these activities. They are valuable in creating experiences with colleagues and peers outside the office setting that can open doors to new and exciting career-changing opportunities.

LESSON 68

EMBRACE YOUR MISTAKES

The CEO of a sales-education company was quoted in The New York Times as saying, "We tell people you've got to love your mistake. If you go through a whole day without making a mistake, you just wasted a whole day because you probably haven't pushed yourself[7]."

Everyone makes mistakes, especially those who are onboarding into a new job or position. Instead of being too cautious on the job, for fear of making a mistake, proceed fearlessly and learn from your failures.

Today's failures are tomorrow's successes. It's why so many companies have embraced a "test and learn" culture so that employees and associates can plan and execute knowing mistakes will be made along the journey.

MAKE YOUR MARK

Learn from your mistakes and apply the learnings to the next challenge, project or activation. You also can ask a mentor or colleague to share moments when they failed to insight into how their careers have evolved.

---

7. https://www.nytimes.com/2016/12/16/business/yuchun-lee-of-allego-the-value-of-a-daily-mistake.html?_r=0

LESSON 69

GET YOURSELF FIRED

Okay, I think I got your attention!

Believe me, I am not advocating for you to get a "pink slip." Instead, take that approach as you ideate how you are going to engage a prospect or secure that first job. When I come across an individual who has a brain lock as they attempt to solve a problem, I simply ask, "What idea will get you fired?" The moment I ask that question, the lock on their brain is removed and their mind races through a stream of creative solutions.

Throughout your career, you will face many times when you "hit the wall" mentally and can't seem to find a solution. Take a moment to think of the most outlandish solution, something that could get you fired, and then dial it back to something that will solve the strategic or creative problem you are trying to solve. This approach to problem solving will help you solve any puzzles throughout your career, enabling you to evolve and advance.

MAKE YOUR MARK

If you are not ready to take this idea yet, when you find yourself staring at the computer screen and nothing is coming, get out of your chair and go for a walk. Take in the buzz around you on the city streets and give in to the rhythm of the day and free your mind.

LESSON 70

THINK BEFORE YOU SPEAK

You are a young executive, full of ideas and eager to please, and you're pretty sure you are ready to contribute in a meeting. But before you blurt out a truly hideous idea and go down in flames, run it by one of your peers or a budding mentor to see if will survive the scrutiny of everyone in the meeting. Make your first attempt at speaking up work for you instead of speaking in circles.

Always organize your thoughts and think before you open your mouth. This applies, whether you are an intern, new on the job or in your 20th year, but the employee with a proven track record can get away with a bad idea while a "newbie" might find themselves on the outside looking in at the next meeting.

Make every word count and have an objective in what you are articulating. You will receive accolades for communicating in a clear and concise manner. It's similar to when we message train a spokesperson before conducting a media interview. Think about the key message you want to deliver and articulate it in as few words as possible.

MAKE YOUR MARK

If you feel like you need a little edge, make notes about what you'd like to say and check them off as you present an idea. It's the ideal way to get used to speaking up in a group setting.

LESSON 71

TAKE A STAND

It can be intimidating to be the newest employee or intern at an organization. It can feel intimidating, so take some time to settle into your role, but don't take so much time to get acclimated that your peers think you have nothing to offer. Don't be shy.

Leave your nerves at the door and make your mark in the role you were hired for. With that, always develop a well-informed point of view and take a stand on issues. The only thing that may be worse than sitting in a team meeting for an hour and not saying anything is not voicing an opinion when asked.

As you become more comfortable in your role, listen carefully, develop a well informed point-of-view and articulate it to your colleagues. You do not want to take the easy route and simply nod in agreement with the group. Instead, demonstrate critical analysis at every opportunity you have even if you agree with the group, provide your unique perspective.

MAKE YOUR MARK

If you can get into the routine early in your career of taking a stand and then confidently articulating it, you will be well served for the next several decades in whatever profession you choose.

LESSON 72

SHOW UP EARLY AND LEAVE LATE

In a course I teach about leadership and communication in organizations, we discuss corporate culture as well as routines that executives get in as part of their organization's culture. In the first week at your new job or internship, observe these routines and take special note of when executives arrive and depart. Once you determine the culturally accepted arrival time for your company, arrive at least 30 minutes early each and every day, get organized and prepare for the day.

In less than a week, your colleagues and managers will take notice. At the end of the day, do the same thing. While this may appear to be a selfish way to impress the boss, it is more about a mindset.

Tom Coughlin, who won two Super Bowls as head coach of the New York Giants, was famous (or infamous with some players) for his five-minute rule. As part of the disciplined approach that he believed ensured success, Coughlin urged players to realize that arriving five minutes ahead of a meeting should be considered "on time" and anything after that was considered "late."

It's no different in the corporate world; arriving early allows you to get organized and prioritize your assignments and deliver assignments ahead of deadline. Staying late allows you to clean up any loose ends that occurred when new priorities infringed on your scheduled tasks for the day; it also gives you the freedom to enjoy the evening because you won't have any work hanging over your head.

MAKE YOUR MARK

It might seem overly rigid to live by these rules, but they will make your life easier and show that you accept the responsibility of being a professional. Arriving early, leaving late and being productive are highly contagious – and establish you as being a natural leader.

LESSON 73

ASK FOR MORE RESPONSIBILITIES

Whether at your first job or internship, always be proactive and ask for additional responsibilities. The young executives who get noticed and recognized are those who raise their hands and ask for more work.

While it seems like a common-sense strategy, you would be surprised how many young executives today finish the assigned task and then dive into their smartphones to catch up on social media and text friends and family.

Instead, after you have completed a deliverable, get out of your cubicle, stretch your legs and poke your head into the offices of your managers and colleagues and simply ask them if you can provide any assistance. You will be surprised by the reaction. First, there will be silence, then a smile will slowly start to spread across their faces and eventually, a light bulb will go off in their head. They are not used to a young intern or executive offering assistance so at first they are in a state of shock. Once they realize what just occurred, they go from shock to happiness and then it dawns on them that they have plenty of work that you could assist them. The next thing you know, you are collaborating with another executive and decision maker in the organization and delivering value in the process. That is a great position to be in.

MAKE YOUR MARK

Once you raise your hand, you are going to have to deliver. If you really want to take on more work, be sure you can handle the duties because you don't want to let anyone down.

LESSON 74

BALANCE WORK AND LIFE

You only have one life – don't waste it away by working all the time.

Corporations, big and small, have made it a priority the past several years to ensure that employees are achieving balance in their lives at work and outside of work. In the long run, it makes us all more effective and productive.

As you settle into that first or second job of your career, try to join a culture that emphasizes a work-life balance. With technology today, you can conduct your work and execute your responsibilities from just about any location. Forward-thinking organizations understand that and promote it.

There is no special award for spending the most time in the office or for being the first person on your team to burn out. Remember, success is a marathon, and that means pacing yourself over the next several decades so that you evolve, improve and become stronger mentally and physically with each passing year.

MAKE YOUR MARK

Achieving a work-life balance and inspiring others to do the same will be incredibly rewarding to you, your colleagues and the organization you work for.

LESSON 75

NEVER TAKE ON AN ASSIGNMENT WITHOUT ASKING QUESTIONS

As an intern or the newest employee in an organization it can be intimidating especially when senior executives task you with an assignment. The natural reaction is to accept the assignment, turn around quickly and get started. A few hours later, you are knee deep in the task and realize you aren't certain that you're doing it correctly.. But as you find yourself faced with a dilemma, you have to make a decision: Do you power on and complete the assignment knowing it may not be what the executive was expecting or do you circle back and ask your questions?

When an intern or entry-level executive starts in my office, I provide them the same guidance and instructions for handling any assignment. I tell them that the first question they should ask is, "Is there a preferred template?" Executives know exactly what format they want when they request a deliverable. They are just too busy or too rushed to tell the individual they are making the request to. The second question centers on timing: "Do you need this in an hour, a day or a week?" By confirming the exacting timing, you can prioritize accordingly. If you only ask those two questions about format and timing, you will be two questions ahead of other individuals at your level.

MAKE YOUR MARK

Never miss the opportunity to ask questions and be sure that you are doing what has been asked of you. It's better to ask questions once than have to keep coming back seeking more answers.

LESSON 76

ALWAYS ASK WHY

If your manager or supervisor makes a request and doesn't explain the "why" behind the request, be sure to ask that one simple, but critical question.

At our agency, we believe it is essential to explain the objective behind a request so that the individual who is handling the deliverable, no matter how big or small, has a complete understanding of why they are conducting research or whatever the assignment is. It not only informs them of the ultimate goal of the assignment but it provides greater context as they are gathering information and they will be more apt to uncover insights that are unexpected.

You will be the recipient of many requests from senior executives. Always be proactive and ask the "why" behind the request if an executive doesn't explain the rationale.

MAKE YOUR MARK

Get in the habit of asking questions. By asking, you will not only have a much better understanding of the assignment but you will be in a better position to deliver results that exceed expectations.

LESSON 77

YOU ARE CREATIVE

No matter the focus of your studies in school or your career path, you are creative.

It amazes me when students are assigned to groups and mention that they are not creative or when I join young executives in a creative brainstorm and some will sit there for 60 minutes and never utter a word.

We are all creative. We can all develop a creative solution to a business challenge. We just need to get out of our comfort zone and be confident in proposing ideas, concepts and solutions. Exercise your creativity as often as you can. It will be one of the most rewarding things you can do in school, at an internship and in your career.

MAKE YOUR MARK

Exercising the right hemisphere of your brain, the creative side, will set your apart from your peers and get you invited to ideation and problem-solving sessions – an invitation that you will never turn down.

LESSON 78

NEVER GET COMFORTABLE

Once you get over the initial anxiety of starting your first internship or job, don't get comfortable with your routine. It is far too easy after you get settled in your job to fall into a routine.

You never want to be comfortable. Instead, it's better to be uncomfortable and restless. If you are just going through the motions, you are no longer evolving and your career growth is quickly coming to a halt. You are like a runner on a treadmill who is going nowhere.

Getting comfortable at your job and your role in an organization will not help you achieve your short and long term career objectives.

MAKE YOUR MARK

As a young executive, you bring into the office dynamic a fresh sensibility. Share your insights because they will likely represent a worldview that hasn't been expressed around a table of veteran employees.

LESSON 79

STAY HUNGRY

The phrase "stay hungry" may sound like the opposite of getting comfortable for young professionals, but it is so much more.

While you want to feel good about your role in the company, you will be smart to maintain a "stay hungry" personal mindset as a reminder to never be satisfied with your work and with your standing in the organization.

Never allow yourself to mix up "comfortable" with "complacent," so master your immediate tasks and be proactive in seeking more responsibilities.

MAKE YOUR MARK

Earn your promotion, your raise, your next job and always look for new opportunities to grow. But don't earn the reputation as a corporate snake. Remember, the business world is smaller than you think, so keep moving forward, but don't build a relationship that has you looking over your shoulder.

LESSON 80

DON'T LET MEETINGS RULE YOUR DAY

Okay, you've got the job. Now, how do you do the job?

When you hear executives say, "I was in meetings all day and didn't get anything accomplished today," use that as motivation to avoid getting stuck on the meeting treadmill that makes it hard to do your job. Young executives typically get invited to many status meetings and calls, but find it hard to raise their hands and say, "Ummm, it's great to be part of the 'synergistic symmetry of strategic sales solutions' session, but that presentation isn't going to write itself. Do you mind if I get back to my cubicle and finish it up?"

If your schedule starts to become meeting heavy on a consistent basis, have a smart, strategic conversation with your manager. Show her that you aren't skipping a meeting to play video games on your laptop, and that you would be more valuable to the team by finishing work that those in the meeting could review as soon as the session breaks up. Then, follow up with your manager to get a download of what you missed in the meeting. They will likely tell you, "Well, you didn't miss much..."

MAKE YOUR MARK

Some executives are addicted to meetings. Avoid getting caught in a cycle of meetings and focus on the priorities that you have been assigned.

LESSON 81

YOU ARE ONLY AS GOOD AS YOUR NEXT WIN

You often hear victorious sports teams say that they will celebrate for 24 hours and then get right back to business.

As you embark on your career, you should adopt that same approach. Always take time to celebrate your wins. However, don't become so intoxicated by your victory that you begin to take your eye off the prize. If you celebrate too long or rely on that last win as your claim to fame, you will be quickly left behind.

MAKE YOUR MARK

For nearly 30 years, I have thrived on one belief: that I will be judged and reviewed by my next win or accomplishment. If you take that approach, you will never be satisfied and will remain hungry throughout your career.

LESSON 82

TRADE MEDIA IS MANDATORY DAILY READING

On the first day that a new intern or employee starts in my office, I provide them a list of more than a dozen marketing trade media outlets and tell them to review their online newsletters every day and call out critical news about brands and campaigns.

Not surprisingly, it is the first time the interns have ever read these marketing trades, but if they want to successfully launch a career in marketing after graduation, it is critical that they make this a daily habit.

No matter what industry you plan to pursue, you need to read the trade media that covers it while you are still in college. Most have free online daily newsletters that you can easily subscribe to. Not only will it help you prepare for your formal job interviews and enable you to become an industry expert, it will get you into a routine that you will continue when you begin your first job. You will also learn at that first job, that most of your colleagues aren't taking quality time to do the same thing. It's like having insider information that no one else is taking advantage of. That's the type of information that will set you up for success.

MAKE YOUR MARK

There is no second prize for ignoring your industry. Information is power and currency in our fast-paced business world and you need to be aware of everything to make informed decisions.

LESSON 83

ONLY BE CONCERNED WITH YOURSELF

While this lesson may sound selfish, it is the complete opposite.

Far too many young executives concern themselves at work with colleagues at their level and their salary, annual bonus and promotions. Instead, put your head down and only be concerned with yourself and the result will be a positive one. Avoid any discussions about other employee's salaries. Nothing good will ever come from it.

Not only is your salary your private business, but spending even a minute thinking about what your colleagues get compensated distracts you from what should be your primary focus at work.

MAKE YOUR MARK

You aren't working for free and you haven't taken a vow of poverty to join the workforce. BUT it's essential that you focus on the tasks at hand. The rest will take care of itself.

LESSON 84

AVOID THE GROUP GOSSIP

Along with not being concerned with your colleague's compensation, don't get caught up in the company gossip. It is a very easy trap to fall into, but leave the gossip to the individuals who will most likely be on their way out the door sooner than later.

While at work, your primary form of "gossip" should be regarding the assignments you have been tasked with and the solutions you and your team are attempting to develop. Any other company gossip regarding co-workers, upper management and the corporate culture should never come out of your mouth. If someone decides to start a conversation with you about such gossip, simply stand up and walk away and let them know you have some pressing deadlines to meet.

MAKE YOUR MARK

Gossip will get you nowhere at work, except potentially in trouble with your managers.

LESSON 85

KEEP YOUR EARS OPEN FOR OPPORTUNITIES

No matter what corporation you work for, always keep your ears open for opportunities where you can lend assistance and support.

While you want to be acutely focused on your responsibilities and your team's objectives, you also want to take a holistic approach to your company's business. For example, at my agency if a team is developing a new-business presentation for a prospect and I am not part of the pitch team, I should still be taking a serious interest. After work and on the weekends, I should proactively experience the brand they will be presenting to and come to work on Monday with any insight I uncovered that could be helpful to their presentation development.

MAKE YOUR MARK

Taking a holistic approach to your job and the organization you work for, will reveal you to be someone who goes above and beyond your day-to-day responsibilities and has the genuine interest in the success of the organization.

LESSON 86

LEAD THE WAY

You are never too young to be a leader.

As you serve your internships and immerse yourself into your first full-time position, don't make the excuse that you are the youngest in the organization or the newest employee. Instead, have the mindset of a leader.

As an intern, emerge as the lead intern through hard work, attention to detail and by taking a confident approach. Individuals are not given leadership roles just because they reach a certain age or have worked at a company for a specific number of years. Individuals earn a leadership role via their consistent actions, performance, results and strategic approach to solving business challenges.

Yes, you can be a leader as a 20-year-old intern or a 22-year-old entry-level account coordinator. From the first day you walk into any organization, evaluate how you can become a leader within that specific culture. Ultimately, that is the role you should aspire to.

MAKE YOUR MARK

Let your leadership skills reveal themselves naturally. It is not about being an opportunist who jumps on the mistakes of others. Rather, be there for support and direction when the time calls for it. Be consistent and dependable and people will know they can count on you.

LESSON 87

COLLABORATION IS CRITICAL

It may seem obvious, but organizations are seeking individuals who have a collaborative spirit and mindset. In other words, they want team players, not executives who like to go it alone. Throughout your career, you will be a member of many teams of various size and make-up. With each and every team, you will want to demonstrate a team-first attitude. It's that attitude that will not only get noticed, but also lead to invitations to join other teams. Of course, you need to back up your collaborative attitude and approach by delivering what the team is relying and depending on you for.

It's critical to consistently demonstrate you are a team player but you need to back that up with your actions. In a team setting, actions speak much louder than words.

MAKE YOUR MARK

Howard Schultz, CEO of Starbucks, said, "Success is best when it is shared." When you possess true leadership skills, you care about the success of the brand, not who gets the credit.

LESSON 88

STRIVE FOR FIVE

As a young executive, you should "Strive for Five." In other words, on a scale of one to five, with five being the highest score, strive to receive a five from your supervisors and managers in everything you do.

If you can keep that simple "Strive for Five" mantra at the forefront of your mind as you go about your business, it will contribute to positive feedback and reviews. If your manager asks you to conduct some basic secondary research, make it extraordinary. Deliver back to them exactly what they asked for and also something extra that provides additional value. If you take that type of approach with everything you do as an intern or full-time employee, you will be well on your way to receiving fives at your next performance review.

MAKE YOUR MARK

By "striving for five," you are setting yourself on a personal path to make a commitment to excellence in every assignment you receive no matter how big or small.

LESSON 89

DON'T CARRY NEGATIVE BAGGAGE TO THE OFFICE

When you open the door and enter your place of work each day, leave all negativity behind. No matter what challenges and conflicts you are facing in your personal and social life, don't bring them to work.

Nothing positive will come at the workplace from someone who decides to come to work with a negative attitude because of something that has nothing to do with work. Negative behavior and communication at the workplace only serves as a distraction and disrupts individuals and teams as they get down to business. Just as a positive attitude is contagious so is a negative one except that its impact can be far-reaching and long lasting.

MAKE YOUR MARK

Coming to work once with a negative attitude is one too many times. An executive who makes a habit of it will soon find themselves on the outside looking in.

LESSON 90

REQUEST CONSTRUCTIVE CRITICISM

Once you get settled into that first full-time position and immerse yourself in your role and responsibilities and your new organization, make it a priority to learn if there is a formal performance review process in place.

I have heard from too many graduates who excitedly start their new job and six months later have no idea how they are progressing. Within your first 30 days, take a proactive approach and request a monthly check-in with your immediate supervisors and managers, even if a formal annual review process exists.

You need to be proactive with your career development and take control of your unique path. No one will do it for you. You are going to want to establish three, six and 12 month goals within your new organization that can serve as your personal metrics for success so that when the time comes for your annual review, you and your mangers already know how you are tracking and there are no surprises. More importantly, you are beginning to map out your career trajectory for your first five years after graduation.

MAKE YOUR MARK

Make it clear to your managers that you are interested in getting regular feedback about your performance because you are dedicated to best serving the company, not because you are looking for personal gratification.

LESSON 91

DON'T FAKE IT 'TIL YOU MAKE IT

I have heard too many executives in the past few years who conduct business via the mantra, "Fake It 'Til You Make it." Whatever you do, please do not become a follower of this philosophy. As a young executive and the new intern or employee at an organization, it would be the easiest route to take. Instead, ask as many questions as possible when you don't understand something and be proactive about what you know and what you don't know.

You will be well received by your new colleagues by asking questions rather than pretending you know what they are discussing or requesting. This especially applies when you receive an assignment from a supervisor or manager. It is best to clarify the assignment and ask questions.

MAKE YOUR MARK

It is smart business and the most efficient and effective way to always seek precise direction and learn your craft. Instead of faking it, be transparent. Believe me, you will earn tremendous respect with that approach.

LESSON 92

TAKE NOTE...AND FILE FOR FUTURE REFERENCE

From your first internship or job interview to every meeting you attend, always take detailed notes. Never attend a meeting, no matter the size, without a pad and pen or your tablet. When a young candidate walks into my office for a job interview, I take note if they are documenting our conversation. They should be. More importantly, as you attend meetings, you will want to take detailed notes and refer to them as you proceed with an assignment or a request.

The key in taking detailed and accurate notes is to listen carefully. If you want to derive even greater value from your note taking, organize your notes after a meeting and proactively submit to your supervisors for review. They will take notice of this extra step.

MAKE YOUR MARK

Taking detailed notes in a business meeting is a lost art. You will set yourself apart by reviving it. More importantly, you will be accurate and confident in how you proceed with the tasks you are asked to perform.

LESSON 93

PRACTICE THE PAUSE

I recently was in a hospital in the waiting area before surgery and a message board with the headline, "Thought of the Week," caught my eye. The message read, "Practice the Pause: Pause before judging whenever you are about to react harshly and you'll avoid doing and saying things you'll reject later."

That message of, "practicing the pause" is applicable to students and graduates seeking their first job or internship and young executives settling into a full-time position. Pause before having a knee-jerk reaction to any communication or messages that you receive from supervisors or potential employers. The natural instinct is to immediately email a response. Instead, draft a response and share with a trusted resource. Even better, consider a face-to-face or phone conversation. Most importantly, pause and develop a well-informed response that is balanced, professional and well written. It will be worth the time and save the drama.

MAKE YOUR MARK

Remember, whatever you write and send by email will never be erased. The recipient can save your response for years to come and use it as a proof point when evaluating your performance or considering you for a promotion.

LESSON 94

PREPARE FOR A PROMOTION

It may seem strange to be providing a lesson about earning a promotion when the focus of this book is your transition from college to your career. However, your first promotion could arrive less than a year at the first organization you work for. With that, while you are handling the responsibilities of your first full-time job, you want to understand what the next role up the ladder requires and begin to ask your manager if you can handle some of those responsibilities.

By planning for a promotion, you are preparing for a successful transition. You do not want to be the young executive who excels in your first role, receives a promotion and can't advance beyond it.

MAKE YOUR MARK

Earning a promotion raises your profile in the company and brings with it a level of new expectations from your supervisors. Preparing for a promotion will ensure that you will make a seamless transition.

LESSON 95

SAYING GOODBYE IS DIFFICULT BUT NECESSARY

This is another lesson that may seem out of place because it has to do with moving on from your first full-time position after graduation and leaving for another organization. While leaving your very first job is difficult based on the professional friendships you have formed, it is only natural for you to be interested in your career evolution. In some cases, you just feel compelled to experience another company and culture. While you are young with few family responsibilities, don't hesitate to take a new opportunity that presents itself.

As I tell young executives all the time when they contemplate a move away from their first job, "You don't want to look back five to 10 years from now and regret that you didn't take advantage of a potential career-changing opportunity."

MAKE YOUR MARK

A job change doesn't always come at the perfect time, but that doesn't mean you shouldn't take it. I made my first move only 10 months into my first job after college. It was my single best career move, because it led me to nearly 30 years at my agency and a collaboration with the best business partners I could have ever hope for.

PART V

THE NEXT 30 YEARS

LESSON 96

CELEBRATE THE WINS

If I have any regrets throughout my career it's that I never took quality time to celebrate the victories along the way. Other than a quick congratulatory team email for winning a new client, I never gathered the team and celebrated our collective accomplishment.

In many cases we not only invested significant time and resources, but we were selected as the winning agency after competitive pitches that featured many agencies. That is something to really celebrate.

MAKE YOUR MARK

From the time you secure your first job, celebrate. Celebrations not only recognize the effort and hustle you and others invested, they commemorate milestones in your career and energize and inspire you to take on the next challenge.

LESSON 97

DON'T FORGET TO HAVE FUN

After you have gone through the arduous process of developing your resumé, securing an internship, expanding your professional network, conducting rounds of interviews and finally securing that first job, don't forget to have fun.

A longtime friend, Bob Babbitt, who wears many hats – writer, publisher, podcaster, marketer, and promoter – in the endurance sports space, authored a book titled, Never A Bad Day. In the introduction, he writes, "Because of the wonderful world of endurance sports and the people who have embraced it, my life has been this awesome journey filled with friends, family, memories and, of course, nothing but great days[8]."

Hopefully, all of us can look back on our careers in the same way Bob reflects on his. While you will work hard, you should have fun along the way so that you can try to follow Babbitt's blueprint for never having a bad day at work.

MAKE YOUR MARK

As you look to secure that first or second job – or any job, now that I think about it – don't just settle for the paycheck. There is not one day that has gone by in my nearly 30-year career that I didn't have fun at work. I have a passion for marketing and creativity and I get to immerse myself in those passions each day at our agency. Make that a priority for your career!

---

8. Babbitt, B. (2013). Never A Bad Day. UK: Meyer & Meyer Sport.

LESSON 98

PAY IT BACK

While I have not officially kept score throughout my career, I appreciate and value other executives who give as much as they take. In other words, if I provide a substantive new business lead to an executive with another organization, I hope that one day they will think of me and pay it back.

We all should be "givers" without attaching strings. I am a big believer that when I perform a good deed for someone in business, sometime in the future, a good deed will be returned. That said, I have dealt with a great number of executives in my career who are unrepentant "takers." As you launch and grow your professional network, secure job interviews and start your career, never forget anyone who went out of their way to help you.

MAKE YOUR MARK

Always keep "givers" top of mind and find a way to return the favor. If you are a "giver" throughout your career, your kindness will be returned many times over. In addition, you would never go wrong by heeding the advice of business icon Malcolm S. Forbes, who said, "You can easily judge the character of a man by how he treats those who can do nothing for him."

LESSON 99

PAY IT FORWARD

It may sound strange to recommend that you start paying it forward, but once you secure and start in your first full-time position, look back and think of all the individuals who provided assistance, big and small, as you starting running your career marathon.

If your journey to your first job is like most graduates, there were many people who contributed. Now, do the same for those who are following in your footsteps. Perhaps there is someone who is a year or two behind you in school who was in some of your courses and is on a similar career path.

Good things will come from paying it forward. Take time to go back to your university to meet with students in your major and share your learnings with them. Be even more proactive and mentor a student as they start to go through the same process you just completed. I tell my students the primary reason I teach is to give back all I have learned over the past three decades.

MAKE YOUR MARK

Your immediate experiences, and the lessons you learned, will be just as valuable as lessons you learn 20 years from now. By establishing ways to help students a year or two behind you, you will deliver tremendous value to them and give them a head start on thinking about their careers.

LESSON 100

NEVER STOP READING

Most graduates think their diploma is the last thing they ever have to read. Trust me, your reading list should grow by the day! Carla Hayden, the 14th librarian of Congress, commented in a New York Times Magazine interview, "If you can absorb information yourself and make your own decisions, that's a freedom[9]." (9)

As you get settled into your first job, read as much as you can about the company you work for to understand who you work for and what their purpose in the business world is.

Now, you need to focus on reading to stay up to date with the competition, to immerse yourself in industry news – and to find new business leads or learn more about potential employers or mentors. I didn't become a voracious reader until I'd earned my master's degree, at the age of 49. I regret that every day.

Today, I read three or more newspapers every morning, as well as all relevant trade publications and popular-culture magazines and books. I absorb information that inspires me to flex my creative and strategic muscles. Reading results in innovative ideas, solutions to business challenges and ultimately, a competitive edge. If I had known this when I graduated from college nearly 30 years ago, I would have started my own reading club.

---

9. Cox, A. M. (2017, January 22). "Carla Hayden Thinks Libraries Are A Key To Freedom". New York Times Magazine, 66.

MAKE YOUR MARK

I also read for fun, as a release and diversion from the everyday world. Going to that oasis also helps open up my subconscious brain

LESSON 101

BE A STUDENT FOR LIFE

As I undertook the challenge of earning my master's degree, it occurred to me that the process of two years of reading, research and writing isn't something I would recommend for everyone on the verge of turning 50 – or even for you at 22. But my first course work in more than 25 years reminded me that there is tremendous value in being a student for life.

The legendary singer Tony Bennett said, "It's best to really study your technique as much as you possibly can so you can have a long career instead of a quick one that's a failure[10]."

Being a student for life means different things to different people. For me, it starts every morning by reading The Wall Street Journal, The New York Times and USA Today to learn about innovative products and ideas, disruptive marketing campaigns and thought leadership from those at the helm of start-ups as well as Fortune 500 companies. It also means taking advantage of every opportunity to learn something new whether via a one-on-one meeting with a mentor or someone you admire or by attending a round-table discussion or a seminar. You will never be able to satisfy your hunger for insights and information, but accept the challenge to continuously and consistently feed that hunger in as many ways as you possibly can.

Your four years of college education follow a formal structure and process and graduation feels like the end of your marathon. But

10. "The Key To Zen For Tony Bennett: Life Is A Gift." (2012, November 20). Retrieved from http://www.npr.org/2012/11/20/165580105/the-key-to-zen-for-tony-bennett-life-is-a-gift

trust me, that was a sprint. Now you have the opportunity to start the next leg of the marathon by designing your own syllabus to support your career evolution. Your customized syllabus can feature as many guest lectures and research projects as you want – or none at all. But now your syllabus should be a living document that has no end but rather an endless series of learning experiences.

Your career will be full of research projects, pop quizzes, debates, peer reviews and exams. You aren't chasing a grade, you're building a career. It will be hard and sometimes it will feel like you are on a treadmill instead of making your way along that marathon route. Just remember this, you are taking the first steps – make them fun, demanding and rewarding.

MAKE YOUR MARK

You will never stop learning no matter what profession you pursue. Instead of taking a reactive approach to advancing in your career, be as proactive as possible in continuously furthering your education and be a student for life.

FINAL THOUGHTS

As I highlight at the beginning of this book, success is a marathon, and so is the career journey that you will take over the next several decades. Enjoy every step along the way, celebrate every milestone, have fun and embrace meeting new and interesting people. I wish you nothing but best wishes for tremendous success in pursuing your passions!

ABOUT THE AUTHOR

Mark Beal is a Managing Partner at Taylor, one of the world's leading consumer public relations agencies, where he started in 1990. Taylor is a brand counselor and public relations partner to a select portfolio of the world's leading consumer brands. Named "Consumer Agency of the Decade" by The Holmes Group, Taylor has partnered with the most influential corporate marketers, utilizing sports, lifestyle, and entertainment platforms to drive consumer engagement. Founded in 1984, Taylor is headquartered in New York and has offices in Los Angeles, Chicago, Atlanta and Charlotte. To learn more about Taylor, visit taylorstrategy.com.

In 2013, Mark was invited by Rutgers University to serve as an adjunct professor in their School of Communication. He has taught 300- and 400-level courses, including Principles of Public Relations, Message Design for Public Relations and Leadership in Groups and Organizations.

Mark received his BA in journalism from Rutgers University and his MA from Kent State University in communications. He lives in Toms River, NJ with his wife, Michele, where they, enjoy boating, paddle boarding, cycling, running, swimming, tennis and golf. They have three children, Drew, Meghan and Summer, and one grandson, Luke.

Twitter: @markbealpr
Email: mbeal@taylorstrategy.com
Phone: +1.212.714.5745

86903225R00083

Made in the USA
Lexington, KY
18 April 2018